BARRON'S PARENTING KEYS

KEYS TO PARENTING THE CHILD WITH AUTISM

Marlene Targ Brill, M.Ed.

W9-AUG-234

BARRON'S

Cover photo by Scott Barrow, Inc., Cold Spring, NY

© Copyright 1994 by Marlene Targ Brill

All inquiries should be addressed to:
Barron's Educational Series, Inc.
250 Wireless Boulevard
Hauppauge, New York 11788

Library of Congress Catalog Card No. 94-12512

International Standard Book No. 0-8120-1679-3

Library of Congress Cataloging-in-Publication Data
Brill, Marlene Targ.
    Keys to parenting the child with autism / Marlene Targ Brill.
        p.   cm. — (Barron's parenting keys)
    Includes bibliographical references and index.
    ISBN 0-8120-1679-3
        1. Autism in children—Popular works. 2. Autistic children—
    Care. 3. Child rearing. 4. Autistic children—Family
    relationships.
        I. Title. II. Series.
RJ506.A9B75   1994
618.92'8982—dc20   94-12512
                                                          CIP

PRINTED IN UNITED STATES OF AMERICA
    7   8800   98765

CONTENTS

INTRODUCTION

A utism can be a fascinating subject, except when it involves your own family. Like an unwelcome guest, a diagnosis of autism can swoop into your lives and change them forever. Even when they suspect something is wrong, few people are ever prepared for hearing that their child has autism.

What does the term mean? What does autism imply for your family or your child's future? Answers to these questions come slowly, because there is no quick fix for any child with autism. The future depends upon severity of symptoms, perseverance, and opportunities to guide your child's progress. Equally important, the future relies on your youngster's ability to find acceptance in a world that often rejects those who are different.

One encouraging note is that your search for assistance comes during a period of heightened disability awareness. Before the 1970s, parents of children with autism rarely received enough information about their children's condition. The few resources available advocated many misconceptions, including blaming parents for their youngster's autism. Professionals held out limited prospects for a child's future and encouraged wholesale placement in institutions to save the child from bad parenting.

The world has advanced since then. Many breakthroughs during the last 30 years led to improved programs for children with autism, helping families cope better. Professionals admitted that biology, rather than rejecting parents, caused the characteristics. Federal and state laws opened doors to early intervention programs and education in schools with nondisabled students. This book is an attempt to help you make sense of what you learn about autism today and give you direction to move forward toward your child's brighter tomorrow.

One parent who was interviewed for this book talked about feeling driven in her attempts to find answers for her child. "Just give us some hope," said another parent. Hope comes from within, but this book may provide the tools to act on your child's behalf in a positive way. Armed with facts and suggestions based on an optimistic, can-do approach, your confidence will rise. I hope this confidence is encouraging.

Keys to Parenting a Child with Autism is arranged in short, readable keys. Each key, or chapter, offers concise information about one aspect of your child's life. You can read one topic or review the entire book or refer to different keys as your child enters each new stage.

Part One, "Understanding Autism," presents the many facets of autism. The keys introduce you to autism and the range of characteristics that encompass the disorder. You read how professionals determine a diagnosis of autism based on myriad clues. You begin to understand why your child's best interests are served when you become and stay informed about autism.

Part Two, "Adjusting to a Child with Autism," deals with the range of feelings families may go through when confronting a life-long disability. This section acknowledges that autism touches every family member—you, your child with autism, other siblings, and the extended family. The effects can be overwhelming. These keys suggest ways to maintain a healthy emotional environment within the family.

Part Three, "Family Supports," can help you realize that you are not alone. You read how to reach out and embrace a new support system that can carry you through the challenges ahead.

Part Four, "The Total Child," lays the groundwork for understanding your child compared with those who learn in traditional ways. You read about physical and mental development and what you can do to foster your child's progress.

Part Five, "Your Child's Learning," concentrates on the education process your child will follow and tips about how to help your child learn better. You discover what the law says about your child's rights to education in the community and your rights as a parent.

Part Six, "Your Older Child With Autism," covers the areas to consider when an adult child prepares to leave home, such as housing, employment, recreation, and the sensitive subject of sex education. This section reinforces the idea that financial and estate planning must be a part of a total commitment to your child's independent community living.

Questions and Answers at the close of the book encapsulate the most commonly requested information about autism. Following this section is a glossary of terms, lists of reading and organization resources, and other appendix material to assist your search for the best services for your child.

Research and technology related to autism are changing rapidly. Therefore, think of this publication as a place to start. I and the people who contributed their recommendations to this book hope that reading these keys will bring you understanding and courage. I wish you and your child with autism a happy, fulfilling life together.

Acknowledgments

I acknowledge the many parents and professionals who gave their time and effort to support this project. Special thanks to professional colleagues Kathryn Moery, Family Resource Center on Disabilities; Veronica Zysk, Autism Society of America; Dr. Donald Meyer, the Sibling Support Project; Dr. Stephen Edelson, the Center for the Study of Autism; Robin Tincha, TASH; Drs. Cathy Lord and Edwin Cook, the University of Chicago; Andrea Freed, Wilmette Public Schools; Dorothy Lucci, Autism Support Center; Lisa Stahurski, Project CHOICES; Susan Moreno, The MAAP; and researchers at the Roeher Institute of Canada.

My heart-felt gratitude to Jeffrey Christenholz, Carol Christenholz, Wallace Christenholz, Cathy Beth, Sue Marengo, Sandy Valentine, Donna Shirley, Barbara Johnson, Stephanie Petkus, and Lindi Mintz for sharing their views on autism and for encouraging this writing.

1

WHAT IS THE CHILD WITH AUTISM LIKE?

Most parents wonder what their new child will be like. How will the child look? Which interests and skills will the baby develop? Now the picture is clouded by autism, however, and you are naturally concerned. To understand the diagnosis, you need facts—facts about autism and about what the label implies.

Autism is a syndrome, rather than a disease that stems from a specific cause. *Syndrome* refers to a cluster of known behaviors that differentiate individuals with and without a disability. In autism, the most affected areas are communication, behavior, and social skills.

Autism is also a *developmental disorder* that influences many aspects of growth, or development. A defect in the way children with autism process information through their senses causes under- or overreaction to the environment. Autistic children withdraw or tantrum to block out disturbing smells, sounds, touch, or movements, thereby missing important interactions that stimulate development.

Your child's autism can be mild, severe, or anywhere in the middle. The extent to which autism affects specific behaviors depends upon your child's makeup. Certain characteristics may remain in some form throughout a child's life. Others, like tantrums, may change with time or fade completely.

A definite diagnosis becomes complicated when symptoms of autism appear in combination with other disabilities. Your child can display limited ability to see, hear, and think and still be autistic. In this case, you may hear the term "*autistic-like*." Children with and without autism show a wide variety of mental abilities and behaviors, and so will your child.

Early Signs

Some parents notice something different about their child at birth. The baby may refuse to suck and looks away when the parent speaks. As time passes, the child may scream continuously without consolation. Your baby may fight washing, dressing, and cuddling longer than the few months of "going through a stage."

Some babies with autism, however, are so quiet they never cry for food. As they mature, they remain uninterested in their surroundings. They never reach for objects, explore with their bodies, or look at other people.

Each type of baby may develop unusual mannerisms. Your child may rock, spin, head bang, or fixate on a rigidly held hand. If your child says words, these may suddenly stop at about 1 to $1^{1}/_{2}$ years. Sometimes, the only communication becomes unexplained tantrums of frustration or pulling you to reach something.

For a long time, you probably wanted to believe sympathetic friends, relatives, and doctors. "He'll grow out of it," they said. Your child only became worse, however. By age three, most affected children show several typical signs of autism. (See "Developmental Symptoms of Autism" in the appendix.)

Communication

Children with autism display a broad range of abilities to speak and understand what they hear. Some children appear deaf because they respond unevenly or not at all to sounds. Many lack verbal and nonverbal communication completely, which only adds to their frustration, or they seem to be speaking in another language.

When talking becomes understandable, some children leave out words or letters. Some children with autism are *echolalic:* they repeat what they overhear. Your child may repeat words, phrases, or sentences immediately after hearing them or at surprisingly inappropriate times. These repetitions may omit the pronoun *I* in response to a request. For example, your child's answer to, Do you want a drink? may be, Do you want a drink?

Children who develop functional language may speak in a monotone. They have difficulty controlling the pitch and intensity of their voices. They rarely volunteer conversation because they are unable to interpret their social world accurately. Consequently, they may repeat commercials or songs as communication.

Studies from the 1980s indicate that about 50 percent of people with autism develop usable speech. More recent research indicates that 83 percent of these children gain language. These figures may change, however, as more children with autism receive structured, quality training at a younger age.

Social Skills

Social deficits distinguish autism from other developmental disabilities and provide one of the most disturbing features of the condition. Your child's inability to relate to other people and situations can be dangerous, embarrassing, and disruptive. Nothing hurts more than a toddler who wriggles away from hugs or refuses eye contact. Parents of older children find obsessional behaviors, tantrums, and self-abuse particularly difficult to deal with, especially from a child who may look physically normal.

Your child with autism may show little interest in making friends, imitating actions, playing with people, or displaying feelings. The child may treat family members and strangers with equal emotion or indifference. Try to understand this seeming disinterest for what it is, an inability to understand social relationships. Your child knows family members and needs your love.

Behavior

Children with autism often prefer to play by themselves. Their play generally lacks imagination and shows inappropriate use of inanimate objects. Your child may become unusually attached to a block or straw or spin a toy car for hours, resisting any attempt to interrupt the activity. This ritualistic behavior is often coupled with obsessive demands for sameness. The slightest change in activity, environment, or schedule can trigger violent outbursts.

A few adults with autism have written about these rituals. (See books by Barron, Grandin, and Williams in *Suggested Reading.*) They report creating *rules* for open doors, clothing, toys, people, or furniture, anything to help them control disorientation from their condition. If anyone broke a rule, they became upset.

Although scientific study has yet to substantiate these accounts, they provide interesting avenues to pursue. Your child may rock, head bang, bite, throw objects, or scream to show dissatisfaction similar to that reported by these authors. Strange play activities or rituals may be your child's way of handling uncomfortable sensations. These adults with autism also recall great pain from heightened senses of sound, light, touch, balance, and taste. Screaming masked unpleasant noises for these people as children, and staying awake at night blocked ringing in the ears or terrifying visions.

Although some senses are magnified for children with autism, others seem deadened. This is why your child with autism may show little fear of real danger. Your youngster may be unable to react to pain appropriately because of a reduced sense of touch. Similarly, the timing of your child's emotions may be inappropriate. You may hear giggles of delight or uncontrollable cries, seemingly without provocation.

Ability to Progress

Parents want to know how much their child can learn. On the one hand, you may see a child who has unusual ability to draw, write, compute facts and numbers, or program computers. (These are called *savant* skills, and researchers have yet to explain them.) On the other hand, your child may refuse toilet training, waving hello, or sitting at the dinner table. What does the future hold for each type of child?

The Autism Society of America reports that 80 percent of people with this lifelong condition test within the moderate to severe range of retardation. Yet, performance on intellectual tests varies with repeated sessions, so these tests remain inconclusive in some instances. (See Key 20 for an in-depth discussion.)

It is important to remember that learning for people with autism continues into adulthood. Children with unusually disruptive behavior may reveal higher intelligence as these behaviors dissipate. Moreover, educators now find that many people with autism have the ability to learn social skills, which are greater indicators of future independence and community acceptance than intelligence tests. With your persistence, early intervention programs, specialized therapy, and quality education, your child's potential is limitless.

Try not to allow your youngster's initial attempts at learning to discourage you. They are unclear predictors of what is to come. For now, enjoy this child, who is more than a cluster of characteristics. Your child with autism is a human being who needs your love and understanding.

2

‹‹

OBTAINING A DIAGNOSIS

C hildren who receive early diagnosis benefit in many ways. Early diagnosis permits eligibility for an array of early intervention and special education services. These services significantly improve autistic behaviors.

Another benefit of early diagnosis is for parents. Now you know the reason for your child's unusual behavior. You can begin to sort out the best procedures to work with your child, and you can locate a support system for yourself.

Autism creates a spectrum of behaviors, some that overlap or mimic other disabilities. To complicate matters, your child may look normal or have advanced motor skills. Therefore, diagnosis can be a long and frustrating process.

Without a specific medical test for autism, professionals usually rely on the presence or absence of certain behaviors to arrive at a diagnosis. This means you and your child may need to visit more places for added tests and to tell your family's story many times. It also means evaluators may differ on your child's exact diagnosis.

As you locate resources to understand your child's behavior, you will probably meet a variety of professionals. Depending upon local resources, some professionals work independently and others are part of a diagnostic, or *multidisciplinary*, team.

School districts and hospital, university, and specialized clinics tend to offer team diagnostic services. The benefits of a team approach are that you receive many services under one roof. In an organized program, one professional, sometimes called the *case manager* or *social worker*, coordinates these efforts to assess your child. This person assists you with the next step once the team presents its findings.

This key focuses on the professionals and evaluation criteria you may encounter while searching for information about this puzzling condition. Review "What Others Want to Know About Your Child" in the appendix to help you prepare for your appointments.

Pediatrician

A pediatrician is probably the first medical resource you consult about concerns. A pediatrician is the primary care physician interested in your child's overall development and, you hope, is well versed about developmental irregularities.

During an evaluation, the pediatrician asks about individual symptoms, such as delayed language, unusual behavior, or impaired social skills; takes family and medical histories; and conducts a complete physical examination. You may be asked to interact with your child for observation.

If indicated, the pediatrician may compare your child's behaviors against diagnostic criteria identified in the *Diagnostic and Statistical Manual of Mental Disorders* (DSM-IV, 1994) and devised by the American Psychiatric Association (APA). The APA is the organization that created new terminology to differentiate autism from psychiatric problems.

You may hear "pervasive developmental disorder" (PDD) as an umbrella term for autism in reference to your child. The pervasive part emphasizes the range of deficits beyond psychological development that are caused by the disability. "Developmental" separates autism from psychological problems that occur later in life.

The 1994 APA criteria revision distinguishes five separate categories of pervasive developmental disorders, including autistic disorder. Another category is PDD not otherwise specified, which includes children who have symptoms similar to but not quite matching other categories. Your child may receive a diagnosis of atypical autism under this category. This means symptoms are severe enough to warrant a diagnosis but not exactly the same as for autism disorder. Some physicians differentiate a high-functioning individual with autism as having Asperger's syndrome, although more research is needed to support this separation.

Figure 1 lists the most recent APA criteria for identifying autism. By reviewing the criteria, you gain some idea of the benchmarks medical personnel follow and the jargon they use. Whatever the label, consider your child's level of functioning and individual characteristics to determine the best treatment.

Without precise tests, autism is frequently mistaken for deafness, severe learning disability, emotional disturbance, delayed language, or mental retardation. Some physicians investigate a diagnosis of autism by *ruling out* these other possible conditions. This method is called *differential diagnosis* and may require the expertise of other professionals.

Pediatric Neurologist

This medical specialist investigates how the brain and nervous system function in children. Neurologists look for seizure activity and coordination problems, such as clumsiness.

Because 25 percent of teenagers with autism develop epilepsy (seizures), the neurologist may recommend an *electroencephalogram (EEG)* for your child. An EEG produces a visual record of electrical impulses discharged by brain cells. When the brain is damaged or a child has epilepsy, the electrical discharges form a pattern characteristic of that disorder.

The test is painless and carries no risk. Because patients must remain still for extended periods of time and cooperate throughout test preparation, your child may need a general anesthetic, which has some hazards.

Psychologist

A psychologist studies human behavior and learning. To evaluate these areas, the psychologist may compare your child's perfor-

Figure 1
DIAGNOSTIC CRITERIA FOR 299.00 AUTISTIC DISORDER*

A. A total of at least six items from (1), (2), and (3), with at least two from (1), and one each from (2) and (3):

   (1) Qualitative impairment in social interaction, as manifested by at least two of the following:

      (a) marked impairment in the use of multiple nonverbal behaviors such as eye-to-eye gaze, facial expression, body postures, and gestures to regulate social interaction.

      (b) failure to develop peer relationships appropriate to developmental level

      (c) a lack of spontaneous seeking to share enjoyment, interests, or achievements with other people (e.g., by a lack of showing, bringing, or pointing out objects of interest)

      (d) lack of social or emotional reciprocity

   (2) Qualitative impairments in communication as manifested by at least one of the following:

      (a) delay in, or total lack of, the development of spoken language (not accompanied by an attempt to compensate through alternative modes of communication such as gesture or mime)

      (b) in individuals with adequate speech, marked impairment in the ability to initiate or sustain a conversation with others

      (c) stereotyped and repetitive use of language or idiosyncratic language

      (d) lack of varied, spontaneous make-believe play or social imitative play appropriate to developmental level

   (3) Restricted repetitive and stereotyped patterns of behavior, interests, and activities, as manifested by at least one of the following:

      (a) encompassing preoccupation with one or more stereotyped and restricted patterns of interest that is abnormal either in intensity or focus

      (b) apparently inflexible adherence to specific, nonfunctional routines or rituals

      (c) stereotyped and repetitive motor mannerisms (e.g., hand or finger flapping or twisting, or complex whole body movements)

      (d) persistent preoccupation with parts of objects

B. Delays or abnormal functioning in at least one of the following areas, with onset prior to age 3 years: (1) social interaction, (2) language as used in social communication, or (3) symbolic or imaginative play.

C. The disturbance is not better accounted for by Rett's Disorder or Childhood Disintegrative Disorder.

*Source: The American Psychiatric Association: *Diagnostic and Statistical Manual of Mental Disorders, Fourth Edition,* Washington, D.C., American Psychiatric Association, 1994. Used with permission.

mance against developmental scales or behavior inventories. You may be asked to verify observations of your child's behavior for these inventories or be observed interacting with your child. Standardized intelligence tests may offer some clues about whether your child has overall delays indicative of retardation or uneven growth, which may imply autism.

Child Psychiatrist

A child psychiatrist looks at many of the same areas of behavior and learning as the psychologist. The difference is that a psychiatrist is a medical doctor with the ability to dispense medicine and integrate information about its reactions.

Speech and Language Pathologist (or Therapist)

A speech and language pathologist assesses hearing and evaluates whether your child's speech and language difficulties derive from autism or another disorder. This information comes from analyzing a child's speech and language, as follows:

Expressive language, the ability to use words, symbols, and gestures to communicate with others

Receptive language, the facility to understand words, symbols, or gestures

Oral-motor functions, your child's use of the tongue, lips, and jaw

Voice quality, the resonance, pitch, articulation, and fluency of speech or other verbal communications

Auditory memory, how well your child recalls information that is heard

General play and work skills, such as attention span and how your child relates to materials and people.

Audiologist

An audiologist is a trained clinician who tests for hearing loss. Audiologists have experience with sophisticated equipment and techniques for evaluating hearing in even very young children. Parents who find their child unresponsive frequently suspect hearing loss, so this is one of the first areas to explore.

Here Are a Few Words of Caution:

- *Try to identify someone who knows about autism and agrees to coordinate your child's program.* Be sure this is someone who doesn't have an interest in one treatment or another.
- *Ask for clarification if you don't understand an explanation or a professional is talking jargon.* You have the right to understand and agree with decisions affecting your child. Remember, you are the consumer.
- *Weigh the value of any test against your child's tolerance and well-being.* Is the information you may obtain worth the trauma to your child, or is it interesting but lacking in relevance to your child's treatment or progress? Never sign permission for any tests you find objectionable to your child's best interests.
- *Watch out for self-fulfilling prophesies among professionals.* Some specialists rely on previous reports without conducting their own evaluation. Helpful information can slip through the cracks because one person assumes the other is correct and beyond question.
- *Remember, the most important reason for seeking a diagnosis is to receive guidance in helping your child.*

3

WHAT CAUSES AUTISM?

The doctors confirm your suspicions: your child has some form of autism. Now you want to know why and how this happened and whether you contributed to your child's symptoms. Unfortunately, the answers you find may be as confusing as your child's diagnosis.

Considerable controversy exists about the exact origins of autism. Recent studies claim a variety of abnormalities that suggest several possible physical causes. Researchers are still investigating abnormal brain scans, infections, genetic differences, hormonal imbalances, and allergic reactions. These avenues suggest some underlying form of neurological or brain dysfunction.

The one origin of autism investigators agree to disregard is the idea that autism results from psychological sources, such as mental illness or faulty child rearing. In other words, *nothing you or your partner did caused your child's autism.*

A Brief History

Children probably exhibited autistic behaviors centuries before Leo Kanner, a psychiatrist at Baltimore's Johns Hopkins University, coined the term in 1943. The Viennese physician Hans Asperger published a description of a similar syndrome the following year. Both men described a special group of children who displayed extreme social deficits, which doctors believed were at the core of the youngsters' disabilities.

Although Kanner suggested biological reasons for the symptoms, both men chose the label "autism," *auto* meaning self, to identify the primary disturbance. The term reflected a symptom of schizophrenia, which was then considered strictly a psychological disorder.

For the next 20 years, researchers erroneously explored child-rearing connections to autism. In 1960, in his book *The Empty Fortress*, Bruno Bettelheim popularized the notion of poor parenting as the reason children developed autism. Based on his conclusions, therapists concocted any number of weird theories for a child's behavior. In one instance, a psychiatrist charged that a four year old remained nonverbal because he rejected his mother, who had been an English major.

A few professionals, especially in France and Italy, still maintain that autism is a mental illness. Take care that you understand these ideas for what they are—historical curiosities.

Brain Disorder

About 33 percent of autistic children have other central nervous system disorders. Recent studies claim differences in the brains of people who have autism. One investigation revealed that the cerebellum is unusually small in autistic patients. This failure to develop may explain why some symptoms of autism, such as changes in language, may occur. Language progresses normally but then vanishes. The brain grows and then stops, like the language that begins and disappears.

The cerebellum controls high-level mental and motor tasks as well as the circuits that regulate attention and the senses. (See Figure 2.) When the circuits are damaged, so are the brain structures in the *limbic system* that are responsible for emotion and behavior. (See Figure 2.) Injury to the limbic system may affect how children with autism relate to other people emotionally.

High-functioning adults with autism have likened the interference caused by damaged circuits to watching television with a poor picture or sound that fades in and out. People with autism are unable to make sense of their world because they receive incomplete sounds and pictures. They may perceive painfully intense perceptions one time and diminished sensations another. Consequently, they miss the social cues and cause-and-effect interactions nonautistic people take for granted.

13

Figure 2
RIGHT SIDE OF THE BRAIN

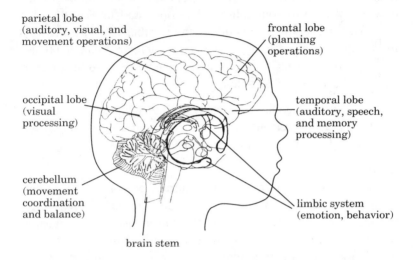

parietal lobe
(auditory, visual, and
movement operations)

frontal lobe
(planning
operations)

occipital lobe
(visual
processing)

temporal lobe
(auditory, speech,
and memory
processing)

cerebellum
(movement
coordination
and balance)

limbic system
(emotion, behavior)

brain stem

Chemical Imbalances

Researchers trace individual autistic symptoms in some children to food allergies or chemical deficiencies in the body. Some literature reports that almost 50 percent of individuals with autism require larger amounts of vitamin B_6. Other studies link autism to hormonal imbalances, elevated levels of certain brain chemicals, such as *opoids*, that decrease pain perception and motivation, and allergies to common foods, such as dairy products, wheat, meat, or sugars. Investigations continue in each of these areas to find more definitive answers. (Consult past issues of *Autism Research Review International* and *Journal of Autism and Developmental Disorders* listed in "Suggested Reading," or contact the Autism Research Institute and Autism Society of America, listed in the Resources, for updated data.)

Hereditary Disorders

Message centers in human body cells, called genes, account for traits of growth, development, and physical characteristics. At conception, a baby receives genes from both parents. When an

14

error occurs in any of these genes, which form microscopic *chromosomes* that are found in every body cell, a genetic disorder may result.

Because genetic makeup regulates brain development, several researchers have explored heredity as a cause of autism. To date, they have discovered that some forms of certain genetic disorders lead to symptoms of autism. Of these, the fragile X syndrome is the most common.

Fragile X accounts for one of ten cases of autism. This newly identified syndrome is the second leading cause of mental retardation behind Down syndrome, another genetic condition. Its name comes from the weak X chromosome (as viewed under the microscope). Besides learning difficulties, children with fragile X often have distinct physical abnormalities, such as large ears, a long nose, and a high forehead.

A genetic component of autism has been researched in several studies of siblings. Findings indicate that the likelihood of autism occurring in the same family twice is 50 to 100 percent greater than expected among healthy siblings. Some research reports a greater incidence of siblings having other learning problems, such as retardation, deafness, or severe learning disabilities. Some studies claim up to 15 percent of siblings have learning difficulties. Among identical twins, those sharing the same genetic material, the incidence of both children having some type of language disorder or intellectual impairment skyrockets to 90 percent.

The genetic components of autism raise as many questions as answers. Even if a single gene for the syndrome is found, this wouldn't explain the majority of cases caused by nongenetic infections, brain damage, or difficult birth. For now, genetics accounts for about 10 percent of cases of autism. Heredity is another direction that needs further study.

Other Possibilities
Factors during and after pregnancy and infections before and after birth can damage the brain. Such diseases as rubella or

cyclomegalovirus, contracted during pregnancy, may pose a threat of autism. Some researchers conclude that complications of brain damage from any number of sources may lead to symptoms of autism. Whatever the cause, however, your child with autism needs the same structured training to stimulate learning, language, and social skills.

4

WHY BE INFORMED?

U nderstanding the implications of autism can be daunting. Some parents react by relentlessly seeking every bit of information about the condition in the hope of finding a cure. Others retreat into their family without benefit or interference from outside influences. Most people fluctuate between these two responses.

Meanwhile, each parent must face the day-to-day needs of the child with autism and deal with the resources within their community. The best way to do this is to be informed.

Make Informed Choices

If you already have a child, you know that parents often receive unsolicited advice. Strangers question your parenting skills with every public tantrum. As the parent of a child with autism, you may encounter even more people who freely offer *their* ideas of what is best for *your* child. You'll meet doctors, therapists, teachers, and family and friends, all with different suggestions.

Most people mean well and consider their information reliable. Current views of autism are relatively new, however. Questionable treatments are conceived yearly. Many people, including some professionals, rely on outdated or inaccurate facts, if they have experienced someone with autism at all. Their recommendations may disagree with your goals for your child and family. To judge what you hear and read fairly, make sure you are informed.

Determine Your Child's Needs

The characteristics of autism change as the child grows and matures. Each stage in your child's development brings new challenges and thoughtful decisions. Are treatment plans working?

Should therapy or classes be changed? Is there another way to handle a given behavior? You know your child best. Therefore, it is your job to assess how your child responds to these experiences and whether the responses are beneficial to your child's overall progress.

At first, your concerns center around understanding your child's unpredictable behavior, aloofness, and means of communication. You want your child to eat, go to the bathroom, and talk independently, skills any parent wants a child to learn.

As the child grows, you worry about social skills. Your child may have a tantrum in response to apparently small actions or may recoil at your touch. How will your child relate to teachers, doctors, or other children? You want your child to learn academics and other practical skills for the future. After high school, the young adult may need help with a smooth transition into the community. You look to evaluate work issues, living arrangements, college, and recreation programs.

At each stage, most children naturally assume more responsibility for decision making on their behalf. The child with autism, however, may always need guidance. To set priorities and make choices, you must know what options are available. You must decide which programs best suit your child's personality and skills at every phase. Your decisions affect the child's ability to become independent, so you must stay informed.

Advocate for Your Child's Best Interests

Always remember that you are your child's greatest advocate. You understand your child's behavior. You invested the most in this person's success. You have the power to influence your child's future, whether or not that future includes autism.

If you are uncomfortable with medication, school, or therapy, find another opinion. One teenager with autism confided that he would have wasted away in an institution had his parents accepted one diagnosis of hopelessness. Be informed, so you understand there is always something you can do to improve life for your child and your family. Trust your judgment.

Examine and weigh the alternatives. Become educated so you can explain autism to friends, teachers, and doctors. Be informed so you have the language and understanding to overcome intimidation should you encounter one of the few professionals who assume the title gives them license to dictate decisions for your child.

Discover You Are Not Alone

One bonus of staying informed is a journey into the community to learn about resources. During your information search, you encounter other parents who have a child with autism. You discover programs that deal with children who have comparable skills, which are staffed by helpful, caring professionals. You find sibling and parent support groups, play groups, professional organizations, many with print materials and large conferences, and university and hospital programs.

In addition to providing information, these groups reinforce the knowledge that you are not alone. You find other parents who confront many of the same issues you face. You can call these parents. You can trade ideas about how to get through a certain stage more easily. You can share everyday joys that only another parent in a similar situation can understand. Being informed makes sense for you, your child, and your family.

5

DEALING WITH YOUR FEELINGS

Y ou may have assumed your baby was healthy. As your infant matured, however, you noticed certain puzzling behaviors. Maybe your baby evaded eye contact or required incredibly little sleep. Perhaps your toddler stopped babbling, fixated on light switches, or rejected your comfort.

Increased suspicions led to an appointment, perhaps several, for evaluation. Without clear-cut answers, your emotions zigzagged with your energy level. Even though you suspected something might be wrong, to hear that your child has some form of lifelong disability can be devastating.

Many professionals and books discuss feelings about being the parent of a child with autism. These resources can't tell you how to feel or for how long. Books like this can provide clues about the range of emotions weathered by others who received similar news. Moreover, they offer suggestions for managing these emotions in ways that may help you cope better.

Understand Your Feelings

Don't be surprised to find yourself overwhelmed by waves of emotions, some so uncharacteristically intense they are scary. Even if you are relieved finally to have a diagnosis, your emotions may seesaw. You may cry, yell, withdraw from everyone, or concentrate on unimportant tasks. You may experience fear, anger, or sadness alternating with pangs of guilt, shame, or jealousy.

These are all normal responses, and they may come and go for a long time. Feelings of "what if" may last a lifetime. Allow these feelings to surface. They need to come out. Without some release, you lose the ability to think clearly at a time when you need energy to understand this special person who relies on you.

The Mourning Process

One of the most difficult tasks is to readjust your thinking about a child you once thought normal. Some parents find adjustment easier if they liken the child's diagnosis to a death in the family. The baby that dies is the idealized baby of their dreams, so they grieve for the loss of their dream baby. Once they finish grieving for their imaginary child, they begin to build new dreams that include the real child who is part of their family.

Grieving is a very personal experience. Each person displays his or her own range and intensity of emotions. Still, your emotional responses may follow a sequence similar to that of others who suffer a great loss.

A common first reaction to autism is shock. You may feel confused or frightened by the label placed on your small child. You question the diagnosis, sometimes searching in vain for another doctor who will tell you something less threatening.

Some parents feel distant from the child. The label suddenly turns this little person they've known since birth into a stranger. Once cherished qualities now seem part of a bizarre pattern.

As the shock subsides, incredible sadness or grief may engulf you, as you mourn the loss of the perfect baby you knew during pregnancy. Guilt develops if you haven't yet accepted that *you did not cause your child's autism*. If your child refuses your attention, you feel rejected even more. Constant unresponsiveness by your child makes you feel incompetent and unwanted.

With time, these feelings may turn into anger toward a demanding baby who leaves you exhausted and upset. Why me? you ask repeatedly. This child may embarrass you when you go out and ignore you at home. You envy parents with healthy children and become annoyed when they seem unaware of how lucky they

21

are. You worried about being a parent: now you may worry how you will ever cope with raising a child with autism.

Without enough accurate information, your mind may jump from one stereotype to another. You fear retardation, psychiatric disorders, or medical complications. You may overreact to seemingly insensitive and unresponsive therapists, doctors, and receptionists who anger you. Your family, friends, and maybe even your child bother you.

Little by little you come to terms with your conflicting emotions. You remember qualities you loved about your baby before the label and between the tantrums. Perhaps the diagnosis helps you understand your child's outbursts better.

The pain may reappear when you least expect it. For now, however, you learn to feel joy in being part of your child's small successes. Gradually, you begin to accept your child and the changes that living with autism brings.

Help Yourself Adjust

Even during the most trying times, you can take steps to help yourself feel better.

- Allow yourself to feel bad. Set aside time to be alone and think about whatever feelings surface. Scream. Grieve. Write in a journal, even if only ten minutes a day. Small amounts of time on a regular basis may be enough to revive your energy to face the stress of parenting a child who seems so unfamiliar.
- Remember, your child is the same little person as before you received the diagnosis. She has talents and skills that are separate from the autism: maybe she draws well, has good balance, or reads. Appreciating these skills may make it easier for you to accept that this is your child, someone who is more than autism.
- Rely on resources that usually sustain you through traumatic situations. Talk with your partner, a friend, a religious leader, or a counselor, anyone who allows you to express your emotions freely.
- Learn about autism. Facts replace worry and inaction. Read small doses of information at a time so you don't become overloaded.

Current reliable facts help you understand your child so you can make more effective decisions for your family. Try to read autobiographies by adults who had severe autism as children. Their paths to independence are illuminating and inspiring. Check "Suggested Reading" for autobiographical and other nonfiction sources.

- Maintain daily routines as much as possible. Routine is a good way to bring order to your family life at a time when you are unable to think about what to do next.

- Choose one or two issues to deal with at a time. Concentrate on only the most important chores that need to be done. Let housework wait. Take leave from work. Give yourself the opportunity to sift through your emotions. You have been hurt deeply. You need time and nurturing to heal.

- Locate other parents of children who have autism. (See Key 11.) They understand what you are going through. They can suggest techniques that worked with their children and can direct you to encouraging resources. Their support during trying times can be a powerful source of reassurance.

- Make decisions carefully. Insist that doctors and therapists explain your child's condition, their jargon, and what the treatments entail. Ask for time to absorb information about medicating your child or enrolling your baby in new programs. Be sure professionals understand that you want to make a difference in your child's life.

6

~~~~~~

YOU AND YOUR PARTNER

Although autism is critical, it doesn't have to reverse the relationship you and your partner worked so hard to build. Many couples discover their marriage strengthened after solving difficult problems together. Their support for each other provides the courage to tackle the continual challenges of raising a child, particularly someone with autism.

At times, the strongest bonds can weaken from the stress of a child born with disabilities. You and your partner may be exhausted from searching for a definite diagnosis or overtired from lack of sleep. Or, you are at different stages of coming to terms with losing the child of your dreams.

Even if you and your partner agree about most aspects of your marriage, you may handle feelings differently now. One of you may be more emotional, the other uncommunicative. One may become totally immersed in learning about autism, the other distant from you and your child. At times, you reverse these reactions as you try to sort out these new and different feelings.

You naturally worry about the unknown—your child's ability to fit into your family and the future of your finances and each family member. These anxieties intensify as you try to maintain a quality relationship and work outside the home.

Couples who have rocky relationships may use autism as an excuse to blame one another for whatever goes wrong at home, possibly even the autism. A partner may exploit the commitment to an unhealthy child as justification for avoiding discussions or time

24

alone with the other person. Differing opinions about therapy may add to the conflict. As tensions build, minor quarrels turn into major disputes.

To prevent damage to your relationship, think about what you can do to ease everyday problems *before* they create open warfare.

Set Times to Talk

Keep lines of communication open, the single best way to solve problems together. Schedule regular uninterrupted sessions to share ideas and talk about emotions. Listen to each other's viewpoint, and try to hear the feelings behind what is said. When you can't agree about something, develop a compromise that you both can handle. You solved problems before the diagnosis: you can still resolve differences and make decisions together.

Regain Your Social Life

For some people withdrawal is a common reaction to stress and exhaustion, yet the most cohesive partners seem to be those who find support from outside interactions. As soon as you are able, try to reclaim your social life. If you are uncomfortable with old friends who seem to have a "normal" family, suggest that couples from your autism support group meet occasionally at a restaurant or bowling alley to socialize. Being with other people as a couple neutralizes the intensity of what you are going through together.

Enjoy Special Times as a Couple

Every parent of a young child reports a lack of time, energy, and money to go out on dates. With many therapy appointments and continual stimulation activities, your personal resources may be stretched to the limit. Scheduling time together can be just as therapeutic as a support group, however.

Give yourself permission to relax and enjoy each other alone. Take the opportunity to discuss life outside children. If money is a problem, ask friends or relatives to care for your child. (See also Key 13.) Share sitting with another parent of a child with autism. If your time is limited, cancel another social obligation, leave evening paperwork at the office one night, or forgo housecleaning for another day. Your relationship is worth it.

Share Responsibilities

All children benefit from both parents' involvement in their care and activities. You chose to produce a child together. Continue the partnership as you raise your youngster with autism. Plan together how to balance these responsibilities with both of your outside obligations. Sharing the load reduces resentment and martyrdom.

Talk regularly about feelings if one parent quits work to stay home with the child. The partner at home may eventually resent the responsibility and long to return to outside work. The working parent may feel isolated from a spouse who devotes too much attention to their child and too little energy to their relationship. Communicate often so you don't drift apart at a time when you most need each other's support.

If you both work outside the home, locate a friend, relative, or paid sitter who can transport your child to early intervention and therapy sessions and practice the exercises. Hire an older child to help you when you are home. As your child's behavior improves, you can arrange day care, possibly in an integrated setting, or consider afterschool or special recreation programs through the local school and park district.

Review Your Finances

A source of conflict for many couples involves money problems that arise from extended diagnostic and treatment sessions for a child with autism. Instead of worrying or fighting about money, try to locate answers to your financial difficulties.

Ask your child's doctors, therapists, and treatment program staff about less expensive alternatives. Many programs have sliding scales or extended payment plans. In some cases, treatment providers can work with your insurance providers to find a code that satisfies coverage.

Learn about the most recent legislation and whether your community offers funding or actual testing and treatment options for your child. (See Keys 24 and 25 about legal rights.) You may also be entitled to government subsidy through Medicare or Medicaid or as a Qualified Medicare Beneficiary. (See also Key 38.)

Should financial concerns become overwhelming, consult a program case manager or financial planner. Contact the Autism Society of America or the Association for Retarded Citizens for resources. If necessary, arrange for a loan to cover special expenses. Don't allow financial problems to erode your relationship.

Monitor Your Relationship Carefully

Consider increased fighting between you and your partner a warning sign. Call for an uninterrupted meeting to explore together what is happening. Agree to try to decide the best way to set your relationship back on course. If you can't interpret or settle your differences, talk with an objective party, such as a friend, marriage counselor, or psychologist.

Plan One Day at a Time

To plan your child's entire life when there are so many unknowns is intimidating and stressful. Learn to tackle problems together, one step at a time. Any more can drive you both into overload. You need to feel success to gain confidence coping with autism. Celebrate your child's achievements together, but remember to appreciate each other as a couple.

7

~~~~~~

BROTHERS AND
SISTERS

Helping siblings to live together happily is a challenge for any parent. Your job may be complicated by the nature of autism. Your children may need to adjust to someone who demands more of their patience and restraint and more of the family's time and attention. The adjustment may be a lifelong process as the needs of all your children change. The two elements that remain constant, however, are your love and sense of fairness.

A Mixed Blessing

Over the past 20 years, researchers have explored the importance of disabilities to the lives of nondisabled siblings. Study results indicate that having a sibling with autism is a mixed blessing. On the positive side, the experience makes many nondisabled individuals more compassionate. They possess a deeper understanding of other people and their differences, and they develop greater appreciation for their own gifts.

The major negative some siblings reported involves facing emotional challenges other children never go through, many similar to what parents experience. By understanding the range of sibling emotions, you can help your nondisabled child adjust better to having a brother or sister with autism.

Understanding Sibling Reactions

A disabled sibling in the family distorts the normal rivalry between sisters and brothers. Competition for attention and individual recognition takes on a different meaning when one sibling plays by different rules. Even the most understanding child eventually resents the constant involvement of therapy sessions or subduing wild outbursts.

Sibling reactions differ according to children's ages and the extent to which autism disrupts family routines. Jealousy is a common reaction to feeling left out. To win parental approval, some younger siblings respond with overattentiveness to the child with autism. Others imitate their autistic brother or sister, such as by bed-wetting. They hope the behaviors that get attention for the sibling with autism will work for them, too.

School-age children may openly resent feeling neglected or burdened with the care of a sibling who displays odd behaviors. They may act out or pick fights at home or at school, believing negative attention is better than none. They may also strive to be perfect to compensate for a sibling's handicaps.

Secret fears may develop at any age. Most arise from misunderstanding. Even your easygoing child may harbor hidden feelings. Sometimes children fear that their parents love the child with a disability more or they worry that autism is contagious, like the flu. They may refuse to ask questions, however, for fear of causing their parents more grief.

By adolescence, siblings may become self-conscious or embarrassed by a relation who is different. At a time when they strive to fit in, they feel saddled with an unusual sibling. They are unsure about how to handle taunts of "idiot," "retard," or "loser" directed at themselves or their sibling. Conflicting emotions arise as they feel anger and embarrassment for their sibling and guilt for being healthy.

Brothers and sisters normally bring out a range of feelings in each other. You can take precautions to ensure healthier adjustment to a sibling with autism.

Handling Feelings
Children look to their parents for ways to deal with autism. If you are loving and caring toward your child with autism, your

other children learn to appreciate their sibling. If you set a tone that respects everyone's feelings, your children are freer to express themselves in a healthy way and to accept each other's individual differences.

Discuss autism before brothers and sisters hear rumblings from people outside your immediate family, and keep your nondisabled children informed. Children sense tension in the family and want to understand what is happening.

Information presented in ways that match their development and abilities helps siblings handle stress better. Reinforce that your child with autism learns, behaves, and communicates differently. Just as siblings were born as they are, the pattern for these differences was probably present at birth.

- Reduce sibling fears. Tell preschoolers they didn't cause their sibling's problems. Similarly, reassure siblings that autism isn't contagious.
- Confirm for older nondisabled siblings that the family made long-term plans for the sibling with autism. They will not be responsible as an adult for a brother or sister with autism.
- Calm siblings' fears about unpredictable outbursts. Reassure siblings of your love and determination to keep all your children and their belongings safe.
- Console siblings that their sibling who has autism isn't rejecting them personally: the autism prevents the child from playing and responding.
- Keep the door open for discussion. Listen to your children without judging what they say. Let them know you care about what they think no matter how negative.
- Help your children find words to express negative emotions and feelings of rejection from a sibling who relates poorly. Role-playing helps some children to identify these feelings. Dramatize your family situation, and exchange roles.
- Allow your nondisabled child to poke, punch, or yell at a picture of your child with autism, or a doll or pillow. Children

with autism are more apt to destroy toys or interrupt play. Your child without autism needs an acceptable outlet for anger that doesn't include hurting another person.

- Watch out for signs of trouble in nondisabled siblings, such as extreme withdrawal, anger, aggression, embarrassment, or constant complaints. You may need to seek outside assistance if these behaviors were uncharacteristic but have become extreme or long-lasting.

- Listen to your child with autism, too. Many parents either concentrate on autistic characteristics or emphasize how ordinary the child is. Neither avenue acknowledges that the child also has differences and fears like any child.

- Spend time with each child separately, even if only for a five-minute talk. Reinforce that you love them and care about their activities.

- Maintain realistic expectations for nondisabled children. You may think that "normal" means problem free compared with autism. Remember that healthy people have unique differences and problems, also.

- Share and switch responsibilities with your partner so that you both spend uninterrupted time with each child.

- Allow your children to resolve their own problems if they bicker for your attention. If fighting becomes unsafe, separate the children for a cooling-off period.

- Bring siblings to therapy or special classes so they understand autism better. Encourage their questions to doctors and therapists. Teach them strategies for working with their sibling to give them confidence.

- Listen to complaints of being teased by outsiders, and help your child understand the feelings involved.

- Practice ways to handle questions and negative comments about a sibling with disabilities. Discuss age-appropriate information about autism to share with friends who tease.

- Encourage your child to feel comfortable about having a sibling with disabilities. Suggest visiting your child's school to talk about autism or inviting children over to learn about what a sibling with autism can do.

31

- Read and talk about stories concerning other children who have siblings with autism. Stories help children understand that others have similar reactions and concerns. (See "Suggested Reading.")
- Locate a support group for your nondisabled child. Siblings deserve the same services as parents. After all, they have the longest relationship with the family member with autism. Local social service agencies (see "Resources") may have sibling groups in which children discuss their concerns in a nonthreatening environment.

Being a sibling involves loving, quarreling, annoying, and embarrassing brothers and sisters. In this respect, your child with autism is like any sibling. With your support, however, all your children will learn to accept each other and establish bonds that last a lifetime.

8

MAKING EACH FAMILY MEMBER SPECIAL

The term *special needs children* evolved to call attention to a segment of our population that was deprived of the same rights as other youngsters. Many communities still need revolutionary labels to give this minority equal consideration. Resist the tendency, however, to imply that the concept suggests "more special" than anyone else in your family.

The basic care, necessities, and personalities of any child alter established patterns within a home, yet attention focused on your special child's behavior, stimulation, and therapy may leave individual family members, parents included, wondering, What about me? I'm special, too!

Set a Positive Tone

As a parent you set the tone for adapting to a family member with autism. From the outset, inform everyone that this child is part of your family rather than the focus of it. He has the same rights as everyone else, but the world can't revolve around him because he has autism. Help everyone accept that the youngster's condition may prove more demanding, but emphasize that these demands will be balanced with those of the entire family.

Recruit Everyone's Support

Nurturing a child with autism requires the energies of every family member. Divide the household workload. Give each person a share he or she can handle, even the child with autism when he is capable. By contributing to running the home, each person feels important and a special part of the family.

Let People Know They Are Special

Every day, find ways to show each family member that he or she is special. Praise your partner and children for well-done tasks, or compliment what they said or how they look. Give hugs, kisses, or treats just for being a special person. Be sure family members know when you need a hug, too.

Do Something for Yourself

How can you nourish others if you feel drained? Set aside time to do something for yourself that helps to restore your energies. Find an activity unrelated to children and autism. Explore a hobby that always attracted your interest, or complete unfinished projects. Establish a daily walking or exercise routine. The most important consideration is that you find something to revitalize your spirit.

Resist the superparent trap that keeps you so scheduled you are without free time. Maintain a steady pace that leaves you enough energy to enjoy your family. Focus on only those activities that must be done. If you like to make lists, record everything you want to do in a day. Prioritize the items on your list in terms of timeliness and necessity. Allow the least urgent activities to wait in favor of doing something for yourself.

Laugh Together

Autism is serious, often causing families great pain. There will come a time, however, when you can gain perspective on your family's situation and regain your sense of humor. Share the silly incidents that involve any of your children. Laugh at some of the embarrassing moments autism creates. Laughing together helps to relieve tension. Best of all, sharing a funny experience shows you can still have fun together.

Play Together

Try to schedule time each week for family activities. Arrange plans around appointments, work, or homework for you, your spouse, or your children. Take turns selecting the family activity, so everyone feels involved and their suggestions valued. Hike in the woods. Roughhouse. Have a tickle session or pillow fight. Make sure everyone participates in the fun. Let everyone know they are special.

9

~~~~~~

A NOTE TO GRANDPARENTS

Remember when you first heard you would be a grandparent, perhaps for the first time? You may have daydreamed about the new baby, just as the parents did, and you envisioned the role you would play in the child's life. None of these visions included any problems.

As your grandchild developed you noticed uncommon behaviors but repressed thoughts that anything was wrong. Now you hear the child has autism, and you are devastated.

Your reactions to the news may vary. So will those of the child's parents. Your relationship with the parents may already be strained because of the pressure of their trying to cope with a difficult or severely withdrawn child. You may worry how everyone will adjust to autism in the family.

By helping yourself first, you become more available to your children at a time when they need you most. Here are some suggestions:

- Permit yourself to feel awful. Give yourself time to go through the same grieving process as your children. Grandparents often grieve twice: once for their child, and once for their grandchild. You may not be the child's parents, but you have been hurt, too. Cry, scream, whatever makes you feel better. Obtain counseling if the grief becomes overpowering. Then, discover ways to support your grandchild's parents.
- Seek current and accurate information about autism. Reliable information eases some of the fears about your grandchild's condition.

Ask a librarian to help you find books and articles concerning autism, or consult organizations listed in Resources. Your children may have literature they want you to read. *Remember,* reject any material that claims that parents cause their child's autism.

- Visit other children who have autism if you live geographically apart from your grandchild. Fear of the unknown is much worse than understanding what autism brings. See for yourself how a family with autism manages, but remember that children with autism vary widely in behavior and abilities.

- Be a good listener for the child's parents. The more severe your grandchild's behavior problems, the more your child needs a nonjudgmental, sympathetic ear on a regular basis. When you visit, combine good listening with an understanding hug.

- Communicate your feelings without trying to take over. Explain to your children that you want to know what is happening, if this is your position. Conversely, if you are concerned about your grand-child, share this with the parents.

Some children try to protect parents. They keep the final diagnosis to themselves, or they try to sound lighthearted when they've just experienced a major disruption. These parents miss out on a grandparent's support, and they make grandparents feel excluded. Raising a child with autism takes the entire family.

- Reassure the parents that you are available should they need you. Then back off. The child's parents have already been through months of worry, and now they need time to deal with the diagnosis of lifelong disability. They need to sort things out for themselves. This is their child.

- Avoid implying in any way that autism came from the parents or in-laws. The parents already feel bad enough and are probably very sensitive to criticism. Besides, such implications are false.

- Be part of your grandchild's development. If you live nearby, accompany the baby to therapy. Learn techniques that are part of your grandchild's treatment. Depending upon your grandchild, the program may include sign language, behavior management techniques, or a picture or electronic communication board. Adapt these techniques to games you would play with any grandchild.

Tell stories. Sing songs. Involvement helps you understand autism and feel more relaxed with a child who may reject affection from everyone.

- Call and let your grandchild hear your voice, if you live out of town. Ask the parents what toys to buy for family visits. Plan together ways to make visits to your home more enjoyable and easier on everyone. For example, you may need to put away your delicate figurine collection or the coffee table with sharp edges if your grandchild has aggressive or abrupt behaviors.

- Follow the rules set by the child's parents. This is particularly important if your grandchild is on a special diet or observes certain rules to control behavior. Watch that you aren't more lenient because the child has a disability.

- Show equal concern for each of your grandchildren. Playing favorites hurts everyone. Be alert that your other grandchildren may feel left out and begin to resent the relative who receives more attention. All children, with or without autism, have feelings and need their grandparents.

- Suggest that your children take some time away from their responsibilities at home. Offer to watch your grandchild with autism or the child's siblings, or hire a trained sitter for them. Prepare a meal or two and bring it over occasionally. Give the parents time to relax, be together uninterrupted, or run errands.

- Be honest if you are uncomfortable interacting with the child. Your grandchild may be stressful to supervise. Admit when emotions are frazzled, including yours. Ask your children to help you learn how to play with a youngster who needs special management. If you are still uneasy with your grandchild but want to help, ask the parents to think of other ways you can support the family.

- Remain involved as your grandchild matures. Discover that this youngster has a unique personality beyond autism. Celebrate your grandchild's accomplishments with the rest of the family. Give the child opportunities to win you over as any grandchild would.

- Accept that your grandchild with autism has a different way of relating that influences development. Understand, however, that this child *will* develop. Delight in these milestones with the family, and enjoy being a grandparent.

10

DEALING WITH OTHER FAMILY, FRIENDS, AND STRANGERS

Anyone close to you already knows something has been troubling you. They see you dealing with a passive or hyperactive child. You rarely call or visit socially because you are too exhausted, busy consulting specialists, or feel isolated from people who seem to have more normal lives. Maybe you talk about troubles easily, maybe not. In either case, you may wonder how you can explain to others what you have difficulty explaining to yourself.

Tell Friends and Family

First of all, you need to be honest. You have nothing to hide, and you did nothing wrong. If you choose, explain that your child has autism, a biological problem that can affect communication, learning, and behavior. This is all you can say or know for certain now.

Manage Reactions

People react differently to serious news. Most are supportive and don't pry beyond what you feel comfortable offering. Some lack the understanding to know what to say, however. They need time to digest what you've said, or they hold outdated views of autism, fears of any disability, or excessive pity for your situation. Here are some ways to help them and yourself:

- Call people before visiting them. Disclosing traumatic information by telephone sometimes gives others a chance to adjust to
the news and deal with their own feelings.
- Photocopy information about autism for family and friends to
read. Review the material for accuracy and myths about the syndrome. Be aware that even the more recent literature from for-
eign countries may still emphasize how parents triggered autism,
although U.S. professionals familiar with autism unanimously
reject this viewpoint. You can locate print and nonprint materials
from many of the resources listed in the appendixes.
- Talk about how you feel. Tell people when you need time to
yourself. Let them know if you feel distraught or confused. Keep
lines of communication open so people understand that you
appreciate their support but want to handle things in your own
way for now.
- Involve others with your child and family. Some friends and relatives are concerned but feel helpless or uncomfortable about
approaching you. Think of jobs they can do for your family.
Allow them to shop, take siblings for a visit, or cook a meal. If
nothing else, suggest that they watch for information about
autism to keep you updated. You would do the same for them.
- Plan times when people can get to know your child. Let them
appreciate that she is a child first, with qualities like any youngster. With time, they will understand that she is an individual
who is more than autism.
- Trust your judgment. Make sure people understand that decisions about your child are your own. Many well-meaning people
believe their advice is best. You may hear that your child should
be in an institution or that there are better treatments. Explain
that you consider all the options, but the decision is yours. For
now, you take one day at a time.
- Avoid wasting energy on strangers' reactions to your child.
Realize that your child's behavior may produce embarrassing
moments or attract attention. Decide ahead if and how you want
to deal with insensitive comments or stares. As you learn to live
with autism, other people's lack of understanding will bother you
less.

- Hold off judging relationships by initial responses to your news. Give people time to become accustomed to knowing someone whose life just turned upside down.
- Admit that friends and priorities change. Some friends and family continue to burden you with their fears, old myths, and stereotypes. When companions cease to be supportive, it's time to find a new support system of people who can empathize and see the positives in your situations, people who can help you manage better.

11

~~~~~~

BUILDING A SUPPORT SYSTEM

Some parents find it difficult to reach out for assistance. They may be unsure about where to turn or hesitate to confront new people. If you are like these people, a good place to start is by contacting individuals who have a child with autism. Approaching one or two people at a time is much less threatening than joining a group or seeking professional advice.

Parent-to-Parent Support

Studies demonstrate that parents who feel supported are less depressed, anxious, and angry. Parents of a child with disabilities provide this support by offering an instant bond. These parents understand your hopes and fears. They reaffirm your parenting skills because they know the challenges firsthand. They can suggest resources to help you get through today while answering questions about what the future may bring. Through parent-to-parent contacts, you discover you are not alone.

Contact the local chapter of the Autism Society of America, the Association for Retarded Citizens (ARC), The Association for Persons with Severe Handicaps (TASH), or the state office of developmental disabilities for parent referrals. Information about national offices for these and other organizations is available from Resources. Local numbers may be listed in your telephone directory.

The National Information Center for Children and Youth with Disabilities (NICHCY), the Roeher Institute (Canada), and the Family Resource Center on Disabilities also provide local contacts who can give you the names of families dealing with autism.

41

Parent Groups

The place where you learned of your child's diagnosis should be able to provide similar direction. Doctors, program social workers, and local school district special education personnel may know parents willing to talk with you.

These parents may invite you to join a parent group. Keep this option open for the future, if you aren't ready for a group now. As your youngster develops, your family's needs may change. A parent group can provide the information and emotional support to meet new challenges.

Each parent group is run differently. Some have discussion sessions and training workshops. Others hold more formal meetings with professional speakers. Larger groups publish regular newsletters, sell current pamphlets, books, and videos, and hold local and national conferences. Their resources can help you and your family through each stage of raising a child with autism.

The federal government sponsors formal parent groups called Parent-To-Parent, Parents-Helping-Parents, or similar names. The NICHCY and Family Resource Center on Disabilities match parents like you with state-sponsored groups across the United States and Canada. *A Parent's Guide to Accessing Parent Groups* from NICHCY details how you can locate or start a group that's right for you.

Historically, parent associations played a key role in advancing services for people with disabilities. Parents lobbied government for laws and funding to give their children equal access to public programs. They organized schools and built sheltered residences and work facilities. More recently, they created training workshops to empower parents with skills to advocate effectively for children who are entering adulthood.

Today, many parent groups comprise influential organizations that function as any other special interest group. Lobbyists contact local government officials or speak with legislators in Washington, D.C. They inform members through newsletters. They organize letter-writing campaigns.

Members of grassroots parent groups understand from their efforts that strength is in numbers. You and your family can benefit from their labor, and you can become as involved as you choose. Along the way, you reach out to others as parents reached out to you. In the process, you can regain lost confidence in your parenting skills, and you begin to build a network of support that can last a lifetime.

12

~~~~~~

SEARCHING FOR PROFESSIONAL SUPPORT

L ocating professional assistance for your family and child with autism is a challenge, one that can be very discouraging. One minute you feel isolated from any resources, the next you drown in a sea of agencies and organizations. How do you sort through the available options to find quality, sympathetic professional support?

One way to reduce the stress of continually seeking services for your child is to organize before you begin. Develop a plan for delving into the social service maze. By giving your search structure, you gain confidence as an individual, a parent, and your child's best advocate.

The National Information Center for Children and Youth with Disabilities suggests the following strategies:

- Decide what you want to ask *before* contacting anyone:

  1. What does your child need?

  2. What does your family need?

  3. What specific answers should come from your conversation or meeting? Do you need parent names, treatment information, therapist referrals, or an advocate to accompany you to an educational planning meeting?

- Write your questions in a notebook, and leave space for responses. Record with whom you spoke, the date, and any notes from the contact. When someone refers you to another person in the same or a different office, remember to ask for the new name and telephone number should you become disconnected. Be sure to note the responses you received. People unable to help you initially may be good resources later.

- Compile a convenient list of resources from your contacts in case you have more questions.
- Keep detailed records of everything that is done with and for your child. Every specialist your child visits will ask about your pregnancy and your child's health, development, past experiences, and treatment. Complete records supply the details you need without relying on your memory. For specifics, review the appendix What Others Want to Know about Your Child.
- Arrange your notes and records into accessible files. Store the information in folders, envelopes, boxes, drawers, or wherever is handy. Little people with disabilities generate big piles of information, so develop a system to categorize the files from the beginning. Separate and label materials regarding medical and dental visits, educational programs, community services, and so on before they take over your home.

Whom to Contact

Many parents are told to check resources in the community but are unclear about what and where these are. Community agencies are public and private agencies in your area that afford various human services. They provide early intervention programs, speech therapy, occupational therapy, special education, recreation, modified housing, adaptive equipment, such as medical care or hearing aids, and counseling.

Your tax dollars fund many of these federal, state, county, or city government programs. Therefore, services are free or for only a small fee. Contact your state office of education, rehabilitation, housing, welfare, or advocacy for the program closest to you.

Private programs supply a similar range of community services. Two larger private agencies concerned with most disabilities are Easter Seal and March of Dimes. These and other private programs offer services for a set fee or on a sliding scale according to family income. If cost is a factor, consider checking with the local school district and insurance company about coverage before ruling out a recommended program.

How to Locate Community Services

A convenient source of telephone numbers and addresses is the telephone directory. Many directories list community services in the front pages. Most separate listings for local, state, and federal government agencies. You can also check specific subject areas, such as physicians or schools, in the buying guide subject index.

Another good resource is the school district. Some states fund school programs for children from birth through adulthood. In areas without resources for babies, contact the local school social worker or superintendent to help you locate agencies that provide these valuable services.

Librarians at public libraries know which parenting and special education books and magazines list contacts as well as publish information. There are so many good publications about autism you can easily find books with copyrights after 1985. Newer books are updated in terms of language, legislation, and research about what your child can accomplish. If you live near a university, contact the special education department or various subject libraries for information and referrals.

When You Still Need Answers

If you have exhausted all the resource options and still need answers, contact the local office of your elected representative. Local and state-level elected officials hire workers to answer voter questions. You can locate your representative's office by looking in the telephone book or calling information assistance. Contact your village or city administration building or the community or high school library to verify the representative's name.

When you make the call, be prepared to ask specific questions and relate how often and from whom you tried and failed to obtain answers. Legislative staff members prefer to intervene on your behalf after you have conducted a thorough inquiry.

When You Live Far from Services

Families who live in remote geographical regions may have problems finding support. In some areas, administrators claim that stretching shrinking resources for a few children is uneconomical, yet too few children for state and federally mandated programs is no excuse to deny someone services. If you live in a remote or rural area, there are sources to contact that specialize in the concerns of isolated families.

- County extension agencies connected with state universities disseminate information about program availability in rural areas.
- The state department of education is responsible by law to assist every school-age citizen.
- The American Council on Rural Special Education (ACRES) is a national nonprofit organization that promotes the interests of rural families with students who require special education. ACRES hosts an annual national conference and disseminates a quarterly newsletter and quarterly journal.
- Some families communicate with professionals in distant areas by citizens band radio, computers, facsimile machines, or videotapes.

The hardest part of your search is getting started, so begin slowly. Plan designated days either to schedule one or two calls or to find answers to one question. If someone can't help you, try elsewhere. Stick with your investigation until you obtain helpful answers to all your questions. Eventually, determination to locate professional support will pay off for you, your child, and your family.

13

RESPITE AND DAY CARE

All parents need time away from the responsibilities of raising their children. This is especially true of parents with children whose disability requires constant supervision and care, sometimes 24 hours a day. Yet, the very people who crave relief the most worry that their child's demands are too stressful to impose on friends, family, or neighborhood babysitters. If this is your situation, the answer to your predicament may be *respite care* or *day care*.

Respite Care

Respite care involves a network of child care and social service agencies that send trained people to provide temporary care. The care is for any child, adolescent, or adult with disabilities. Depending upon services in your area, you can arrange sitting for several hours so that you can run errands, for overnight, or for several weeks for a family vacation. Respite care gives you the peace of mind of knowing your child is in capable hands.

Acknowledgment of the need for respite care surfaced during the 1970s. A few years earlier, legislation authorized individuals with disabilities to live in the least restrictive environment. Thousands of unprepared residents left institutions to live in the community with their families.

Over time, professionals watched these families deteriorate from the stress of the continual long-term care of a family member. They observed, however, that the slightest relief from responsibility revived family members and energized their relationships.

Respite care gained support at the government level after passage of the Children's Justice Act (Public Law 99-401) in 1986 and its amendment, Public Law 101-127, the Children with Disabilities Temporary Care Reauthorization Act. The legislation approved grants for states to develop and implement affordable respite care programs and crisis nurseries.

Families soon discovered that the law fell short of providing national guidelines for respite care. Every state dispensed different versions of the service, and individual agencies devised their own criteria for length of time and funding allotments. Competition and long waiting lists were problems from the start. Once again, parents had to be persistent to find the right respite care for their family.

Depending upon local availability, your respite care may involve the following:

Individual in-home services by trained sitters
Companions to accompany your child to recreational activities
Residential care for short-term placement, as in hospitals, nursing care residences, or foster care
Summer camp
Flexible funding, whereby your family identifies what it needs and you apply a funding allotment to the applicable service

To determine respite options in your area, talk with staff at your child's program or local school. Ask other parents, or contact local chapters of the Autism Society of America or the Association for Retarded Citizens. Contact the Texas Respite Resource Network for information about the nearest respite agency, the National Information Center for Children and Youth with Disabilities for their *state resource sheet*, or the local or national Lekotek center.

You may have to be creative about locating respite services. Some areas have YMCAs, groups of retired individuals, Camp Fire Boys and Girls, Foster Grandparents, or Big Brother and Big Sister

KEYS TO PARENTING THE CHILD WITH AUTISM

programs that assist families with respite care. Nursing schools and babysitting, nursing, and hospice services all train staff to manage someone with special needs. If you live near a university or college, ask whether any special education or psychology students are interested in babysitting.

Day Care

Day care is an option for parents who need regular or long-term care for a child with special needs. Parents view day care as an opportunity for their child with autism to be exposed to the same social interactions as other children. Day care can be your child's first step toward integrated education. (See Key 30.)

The problem, however, is finding day care that will take your child. Few day care centers or preschools have the expertise to handle a youngster with unusual behavior. Still, inexperience is no excuse under the Americans for Disabilities Act (ADA), which states that discrimination of this kind is illegal. Because there is no ADA police force, however, inclusion comes only after one family files a law suit against the discriminating agency.

The National Information Center for Children and Youth with Disabilities offers other ways to work with day care providers so they feel comfortable with your child:

- Be honest about your child's needs. Tell day care providers how much special attention your child requires.
- Offer to stay on-site initially to help your child and the staff adjust.
- Provide printed information about autism so teachers can read for themselves what to expect.
- Offer to help staff locate respite providers to accompany your child to day care.
- Locate a state inclusion trainer through the state department of education to train staff in the skills needed to handle someone who is unfamiliar and help ease your child into the setting.

Investigate respite and day care services whether you need them now or not, because many providers have long waiting lists.

This way, you have coverage for your child with autism in case of a family emergency or an opportunity for spontaneous fun. The primary concern is for you to feel comfortable with your child's care. Then you, your spouse, and your other children can relax and enjoy your time together.

14

DECIDING TO HAVE ANOTHER CHILD

Should we have another child? is a question asked by many anxious parents of a child with autism, and the answer doesn't come easily. One parent worries about the extra workload and financial burdens. Another wonders about the impact on their child with a disability. Most parents struggle with the gravest concern—the prospect of bringing another child with autism into the family.

Guidebooks and counsel from those close to you give some direction, but they cannot settle these critical issues for you. The ultimate decision is between you and your partner. Still, there are considerations that can help you decide.

Weigh the Options

Expanding the family is a major decision for any couple, whether or not they have a disabled child. In your situation, the extent of your child's autism increases the amount of time, energy, and money you spend beyond that for the average raising of a child. Then the real question becomes, Do you have the added emotional, physical, and financial resources to handle another child and still be fair to your first child, yourself, and your partner?

Talk with other parents who have raised more than one child. Find out how a new baby changed their lives. Did the baby interest the child with autism and provide increased stimulation, which would ease your job? Or did safety become an issue because of unpredictable violent rages? Other parents can help you learn what to look for and how to prevent difficult situations before an infant arrives, should another child be your choice.

Evaluate the Risks

Unfortunately, the risks associated with conceiving another child with autism are far from clear-cut. A major stumbling block is that autism is a disability without a common cause. Even when a physician finds specific damage or an imbalance to explain your child's autistic symptoms, the exact reason for the impairment may remain a mystery.

The chances of another baby with autism depend on two major factors: a family history of autism and related conditions and the type of autism your child has, if this can be determined. Ask your pediatrician for the name of a geneticist to help you examine the risk factors. *Geneticists* are scientists who study human genetics and are well versed in the latest clues to this puzzling disability.

Currently, the incidence of autism ranges from 5 to 15 per 10,000 births, depending upon the criterion measured. Of these children, between 2 and 3 percent have siblings who show similar symptoms, and another 10 to 15 percent reveal other significant learning problems. These figures translate into 50 to 100 times that in the general population.

Some geneticists estimate the overall recurrent risk for certain autistic features as 8 to 9 percent, with females at greater risk as carriers. The risk of passing on autism as part of another genetic, metabolic, or neurological disorder is greater when autism is already present in one child.

In children who have the genetic abnormality fragile X syndrome, the chances of a sibling with autism increase by almost 50 percent. Not all children with fragile X have autistic features, however, and fragile X accounts for only 10 percent of the cases of autism. However, the numbers support further exploration when making such an important decision as having another child.

Talk with the geneticist about giving your child with autism a blood test to rule out fragile X syndrome and other hereditary causes. The results, although not foolproof, will help you evaluate a predisposition to autism. Although both males and females can carry the fragile X gene, they may or may not show features of fragile X or autism. Because girls have two X genes, one gene can mask symptoms produced by the defective gene. This is why boys tend to show more symptoms of fragile X and associated autism.

Should tests reveal this tendency but you decide to conceive another child, there are ways that you can determine during pregnancy whether your unborn baby has the fragile X gene. As yet, tests cannot determine whether the fetus will show autistic symptoms or be a carrier.

> *Amniocentesis* is a common medical procedure to test abnormal chromosomes. With amniocentesis, a technician inserts a needle through the abdomen into the uterus and draws amniotic fluid, the liquid surrounding the fetus, for analysis. The procedure usually occurs between 16 and 18 weeks of pregnancy, and it carries a 1 in 200 risk of miscarriage.
>
> *Chorionic villus sampling (CVS)* is a newer method of analyzing chromosomes between weeks 8 and 11. With this test, doctors insert a needle either through the vagina and cervix or through the abdomen. The needle withdraws cells from the maturing *placenta*, the sac protecting the fetus, for evaluation. CVS causes spontaneous abortion in about 1 in 100 women and possible deformities in anywhere from 1 in 100 to 1 in 1,000 babies.

The advantage of CVS is the earlier detection of genetic disorders during pregnancy. If tests prove positive, a woman has the option of choosing a safer first-trimester abortion. Parents then grapple with the painful decision of whether to terminate the pregnancy.

Judgments about childbirth require many tough decisions, particularly when autism is involved. To simplify your decision-making journey, think about your entire family. Assess whether the benefits of self-confidence and balance a healthy child can bring offset the challenges. Envision how each person would react to the addition of another child, someone probably without a disability.

15

WORKING WITH THE
MEDICAL COMMUNITY

Y ou and your child's medical professionals agree that a healthy
person copes better with life. With their skills and your dedi-
cation, you work toward a common goal of keeping your child
well. This teamwork is important to your youngster's progress.

At times, however, interactions concerning someone with
autism can become emotionally charged. Small misunderstandings
by either party may trigger obstacles to effective treatment. Your
child's irregular behavior may add tension to strained office visits.
To promote positive parent-professional relations and reduce
stress, consider some preventive measures.

Flexibility Counts
Autism may influence any area of development. Therefore,
you need a physician who is knowledgeable about the syndrome
and its effects. Moreover, this person must be comfortable with
children and willing to adjust to someone who requires special
handling.

Call a doctor's office before committing to an appointment.
Ask a nurse if the doctor treats children with autism. Establish the
doctor's credentials, fees, insurance considerations, and appointment policies. Determine the size of the practice. A smaller practice allows your child to become accustomed more easily to the
people and surroundings. Familiarity will make your child less
fearful.

Talk with the doctor, too. You and your spouse may want to
interview this person without your child. Decide whether the

physician is willing to work with you to make visits less traumatic for the child. Is the doctor uncomfortable with your questions? Are responses understandable? What approach does the doctor suggest for examining an anxious child?

Most important, question the physician's beliefs about autism. If the doctor is convinced that parents cause their child's problems, contact someone else.

About Appointments

The chief complaints of parents concern the amount of time spent waiting for appointments and the elaborate office procedures. Most children dislike delays, but your child with autism may find the slightest wait unbearable. Here are some suggestions to reduce frustration for you and your child:

- Schedule appointments for when your child is more adaptable—morning or afternoon or before or after a meal. Otherwise, request the first appointment of the day or after lunch to reduce waiting time from patient backlog. If your doctor is part of a clinic, ask at which time of the day there are the fewest patients.
- Call before leaving home to see if the doctor is on schedule or an emergency has arisen that would delay your appointment. Then, be sure to be on time yourself.
- Arrange the number and length of appointments your child can handle. Sometimes children need several sessions with doctors and technicians. Decide whether your child performs better with a cluster of appointments on one day or scattered appointments. Which can you handle better: one long stressful day or several shorter sessions, possibly each with outbursts?
- Prepare your child for what will happen. This will help to reduce anxiety. Incorporate the doctor's visit into your child's behavior modification routine. (See Key 22.) Identify the behaviors that must occur and your child's reward for these behaviors. Offer rewards at intervals that will satisfy your child. Praise your child continuously for good waiting behavior.
- Ask for a quiet examining room to wait in if your child becomes too excitable to stay in the waiting area.

- Plan ahead for a restless child. Even with the best preparations, you may still encounter delays. Bring a favorite toy or object to ease your child's wait. Occupy waiting time with special activities together. Pack snacks for an extra long wait.

During Sessions

For a new doctor or therapist, bring copies of insurance forms for billing and past records or brain scans of your child. Some physicians charge for reproducing records or require written requests, which takes time.

Help your child adjust to the doctor. Remind the physician to move slowly. Ask if your child can handle instruments and just get to know the doctor for awhile before an examination.

To extract the most information from physician's visits, bring a prepared list of questions. Carry extra pens and paper to write answers and take notes. Ask the professional for printed information to explain further what is said. Disturbing or complicated news is difficult to digest in one session.

Request as much information as you need to understand and plan for your child. Never allow a professional to unnerve you or cut you short. You have a right to explanations in understandable terms. You are the consumer.

Children rarely enjoy sitting through adult conversations. Your child with autism may be even more distracted. Take someone with you to the appointment who can keep the child busy while you talk with the doctor, or ask if a nurse can supervise your child out of the office. You may need to schedule another appointment or telephone call to talk without interruption.

Telephone Manners

Waiting for a doctor's telephone call can be frustrating. Nurses can frequently answer questions or furnish test results, but you still may need the doctor for interpretation.

Ask the receptionist when the doctor usually calls patients. Some doctors return nonemergency calls at a given time, such

57

as during lunch; others wait until after hours. Be sure to keep the telephone free at the appointed hour.

Similarly, tell the receptionist whether you will be at another number or unavailable for calls. This way, the doctor can save time on failed attempts to call you, and you can still leave the telephone.

When the doctor or therapist calls, be prepared with necessary information and questions to ask. If there are new developments, share them. If you discovered something unusual, follow your intuition. Be an informed and informative partner on your child's professional team.

16

^^^

YOUR CHILD'S
OVERALL HEALTH

All children acquire their share of medical problems. Childhood diseases, infections, and scrapes come and go throughout early and adolescent years. With autism, however, these relatively minor irritations sometimes contribute to major behavior disturbances or developmental delays. Your child may be unable to communicate physical discomfort. If your child fears new people or situations or resists touch, this may interfere with a doctor's ability to assess health status.

Preventive Medicine

To help your child stay healthy, take him for regular examinations before problems occur. Allow your child and a physician who understands autism to become comfortable with each other so that correctable medical situations can be remedied early. Suggest that the doctor keep detailed anecdotal records. Any behavioral changes between visits may indicate a change in health.

At home, role play with your child about going to the doctor. Use pictures, computers, or dolls, anything to make a doctor's visit more meaningful and give your child words or behaviors to describe physical feelings. Observe your child at home for abrupt behavioral changes that may suggest illness.

A child with autism requires the same routine immunizations and screenings as any child. Table 1 indicates a schedule of examinations and inoculations recommended by the American Academy of Pediatrics. Because the senses may be heightened or depressed from autism, you may want to have comprehensive hearing and vision tests administered more frequently.

Table 1
IMMUNIZATION AND EXAMINATION RECOMMENDATIONS*

Procedures	Months									Years										
	1	2	4	6	9	12	15	18	24	3	4	5	6	8	10	12	14	16	18	20+
Measurements																				
Height and weight	✓	✓	✓	✓	✓	✓	✓	✓	✓	✓	✓	✓	✓	✓	✓	✓	✓	✓	✓	✓
Head size	✓	✓	✓	✓	✓	✓	✓	✓												
Blood pressure										✓	✓	✓	✓	✓	✓	✓	✓	✓	✓	✓
Sensory screening, vision and hearing	(At diagnosis and as needed)																			
Development and behavioral assessment	✓	✓	✓	✓	✓	✓	✓	✓	✓	✓	✓	✓	✓	✓	✓	✓	✓	✓	✓	✓
Physical examination	✓	✓	✓	✓	✓	✓	✓	✓	✓	✓	✓	✓	✓	✓	✓	✓	✓	✓	✓	✓
Metabolic screen: Thyroid, PKU, etc.	✓									(At diagnosis and as needed)										
Blood tests (as needed)					✓				✓					✓					✓	
Urinalysis (as needed)				✓					✓					✓					✓	
Immunizations																				
Tuberculin						✓			✓										✓	
DTP		✓	✓	✓				✓			✓									
Polio		✓	✓					✓				✓								
MMR							✓									✓				
Tetanus–diphtheria																	✓			
Dental										✓	✓	✓	✓	✓	✓	✓	✓	✓	✓	✓

*Adapted from the American Academy of Pediatrics and *Keys to Parenting a Child with Down Syndrome*, p. 52.

In addition, your physician may order a blood sample to screen for chromosome abnormalities and blood and urine samples to test for hormonal imbalances. Information from each screening should be weighed against your child's comfort level and ability to handle intrusive testing.

A Word of Caution

Certain physical disturbances occur more often in conjunction with autism, especially when other disabilities are involved. These concerns are important for you to recognize, even though not every child with autism experiences them.

Epilepsy

Epilepsy, or seizures, occurs in about 25 percent of children with autism. For unknown reasons, seizures develop more frequently in adolescents and in nonverbal and lower functioning children.

Epilepsy comes from abnormal electrical charges within the brain. Seizure activity distresses the nervous system, causing temporary mild to severe reactions. A child may blink, stare, or black out for a few minutes. During a full, or *grand mal*, seizure the child may fall, stiffen, move uncontrollably, have difficulty breathing, turn pale, drool, or lose bladder or bowel control.

Doctors diagnose epilepsy through medical examination and medical history and by ordering an electroencephalogram (EEG). The EEG is a test that shows a visual picture of the brain's electrical activity, but it is sometimes inconclusive. Some individuals have epilepsy and show normal EEGs, and vice versa.

When seizures are infrequent, your physician may choose a wait-and-see approach and determine severity. More commonly, your child will receive *anticonvulsant* medication to control the seizures. Anticonvulsants are strong drugs, so the doctor should monitor your child closely for side effects, such as altered blood chemistry, swollen gums, or extreme sleepiness.

Should your child experience a seizure, *Stay Calm*. Never restrain the child or force something into the mouth. The idea that people with seizures swallow their tongues is false. You can help your child by clearing the area of hard or sharp objects. If you can move close without harming your child or yourself, remove eyeglasses or loosen tight clothing. Otherwise, leave your child alone. The seizure will run its course in less than two minutes.

After a seizure, turn your child to one side to allow his mouth to drain. He may be confused or extremely tired and need sleep. Stay close until he awakens fully and is reoriented. Call for an ambulance or the police if breathing fails to resume or your child seizures repeatedly.

Other Neurological Disturbances

Your child may be more prone to immature reflexes or *nystagmus*, involuntary rapid eye movement. Abnormal nystagmus results from insufficient stimulation to the eye, inner ear disturbances, or nervous system disorder in the part of the brain responsible for eye movements and coordination. Nystagmus can affect vision or balance, but treatment depends upon the underlying cause.

Dental Care

Routine dental examinations are particularly important for someone who receives seizure medicine and who resists toothbrushing for any number of reasons. Choose a dentist who can work with your child until he feels comfortable with dental procedures. This may take several minivisits. If your child is uncooperative, he may need general anesthesia in extreme situations. Try to limit the amount of sweets in your child's diet before cavities develop.

Keep trying to encourage good oral hygiene at home. Perhaps your child tolerates water with fluoride or bubblegum toothpaste. If nothing else, serve your child hard fruits and vegetables, such as apples or carrots, that clean particles from between teeth.

Nutrition

Children with autism sometimes have unusual eating habits beyond those displayed by healthy but fussy youngsters. Some children may refuse new tastes or textures or may eat compulsively. Others may lack the muscle control to chew more demanding foods.

Specialists may be helpful with nutrition questions. A speech and language pathologist can determine whether oral muscles are working properly. Your physician can rule out physical illness or medication as a cause of over- or undereating.

You can also review your child's eating habits with a *nutritionist*, who can evaluate whether he ingests enough vitamins and minerals for growth. The nutritionist may suggest foods that are acceptable to your child and nutritionally sound. Here are some suggestions for changing rigid or excessive eating habits that result from nonphysical causes:

• Introduce a new food that is similar to a familiar food, and mix new foods with old.
• Prepare the same foods as for the rest of the family. Try not to react and place importance on food if your child won't eat. Missing a meal or two is okay. Your child will be more apt to eat what you serve at the next meal.
• Reduce the amount of sweet or fatty foods you buy. Monitor your child's diet as you would any child's.

Injuries

Children normally fall or hurt themselves. Your child may be more susceptible to accidents because of poor judgment and dangerous habits. The resulting bruises can lead to infection when the child irritates the injury or can't tell you a sore refuses to heal. Prepare to child proof your home longer than for other youngsters to avoid injury:

• Remove lead-based paints and crayons, especially with a child who mouths everything.
• Fix wallpaper that has unglued, eye-catching folds. Paper eaters rip paper from walls.
• Lock doors to cabinets and closets that hold sharp, poisonous, small, or dangerous objects. Place safety hooks on cabinet doors and covers on door handles. These are available from hardware stores.
• Cover electrical sockets and ensure that the tiny covers are unattractive to your child.

- Check window frames and loose window screens. Nimble fingers can open latches more easily than you think.
- Check that plants and added fertilizers are nonpoisonous in case your child experiments with a new taste treat.
- Keep emergency numbers visible for quick access, including the local poison control center.
- Stock first-aid and antipoison kits. These are available from the local pharmacy or poison control center.
- Encourage your child to swim and learn respect for water.
- Show neighbors where you live and introduce them to your child, if he is a wanderer.
- Use back burners on the stove, and teach the meaning of *hot* early.
- Place stickers on clear glass that is at eye level.
- Rule out pain from infection when dealing with new self-abusive behavior, such as head banging from an ear infection.
- Learn behavioral management techniques to reduce other self-injuries from head banging and repeated hitting and scratching.
- Consider a helmet for head banging and gloves for a child who scratches compulsively.

A few extra precautions will protect your child with autism for a long, healthy life and make your parenting job easier.

17

~~~~~~

MEDICATIONS
AND DIET

As a concerned parent, you want your child to have every opportunity to progress. Your physician suggests medication or a specific diet. Maybe your mind races back to the days when doctors overmedicated people in institutions to calm them for overburdened staffs. Perhaps you view medication and diet as cure-alls. Whichever the case, you need the facts to judge for yourself and your child.

Diet

During the 1960s and 1970s, several researchers believed certain characteristics, such as hyperactivity, were linked to food additives and sugars. To date, scientific studies have failed to connect behavior with food choices. There are so many unknowns, however, that the parents of any child are wise to follow healthy nutritional guidelines that call for serving natural fruits, vegetables, and grains and limiting sugars, fats, and additives, such as preservatives, flavor enhancers, and colorings.

Medication

The question of prescribing medication to combat autism is complex. Children with autism have such varying symptoms that they respond inconsistently to medication. Some parents report major reductions in specific disturbing behaviors after a short time on medication. Others warn of serious side effects.

One problem with any medication plan is your child's inability to report reactions, such as feeling dizzy or having blurred vision. Consider the following guidelines when your child's physician recommends medication.

Review Reasons for Medication

Try to view medication as just another option. Medications cannot cure autism, but they can benefit some children. Think of medication as support, rather than replacement, of your child's structured behavior management program.

Your physician may recommend medication when your child experiences the following behaviors:

Self-abuse, such as head banging, eventually causing damage
Frequent aggressive behavior outbursts
Repetitive or overactive behaviors that severely interfere
    with learning and social interactions
Inability to sleep for sustained periods of time
Repeated seizures

Evaluate Side Effects and Possible Risks

All medications have advantages and disadvantages. What works for one child may bother your child. A medication that produces rare side effects at one dose may cause harm at another. Sometimes, favorable prescriptions turn unhealthy when taken for a long time. You and the physician must therefore weigh carefully each medication choice and dosage.

Neuroleptics

The most common class of medications prescribed for autistic symptoms are the *neuroleptics, major tranquilizers,* or *antipsychotics.* Neuroleptics suppress the action of *dopamine,* a chemical that transmits impulses between nerve cells. Levels of dopamine influence motor skills, thought processes, and emotions.

Typical major tranquilizers are haloperidol (Haldol), chlorpromazine (Thorazine), trifluoperazine (Stelazine), and thiothixene (Navane). Various forms of these drugs appear to reduce self-abuse and repeated motor behaviors and to increase attention span. Several studies verify that these medications also reduce hyperactivity, impulsiveness, and social detachment.

The most common side effects of neuroleptics are blurred vision, dry mouth, muscle spasms, and constipation. Some children become so sleepy they are unable to learn. Long-term treatment with neuroleptics can cause damage to the very structures they try to heal, the nervous system. Children may develop odd body movements, even after medication ends, but these are reversible.

A serious side effect for as many as 20 to 25 percent of children who take neuroleptics is *tardive dyskinesia*, which can be irreversible. In this condition, rapid involuntary body movements accompany contortions of facial muscles. Tardive dyskinesia is more common after extended treatment, so your child must be observed closely after stopping the medication.

Fenfluramine

Fenfluramine is under study to reduce levels of *serotonin*, a chemical in the blood. For unknown reasons, elevated serotonin levels have been detected in 33 percent of people with autism. A few researchers claim that fenfluramine treatment results in improved social skills, learning, and behavior. Some side effects from the drug are sleepiness, appetite reduction, and irritability, although tests of large doses on animals show brain damage as well.

Stimulants and Minor Tranquilizers

Minor tranquilizers, such as synthetic Valium and Librium, are generally ineffective for symptoms of autism. They may prove helpful in older children to reduce anxiety. Difficulties arise, however, when tranquilizers contribute to the increased isolation of a normally withdrawn child.

Stimulants, which have traditionally been prescribed for hyperactivity, have little effect on children with autism. Because children with autism react unpredictably to medicines, stimulants often increase the behaviors they are meant to suppress.

Vitamin Therapy

Studies advocating large doses of vitamins and minerals, such as B_6, zinc, and magnesium, and special diets reveal inconclusive results. Some parents report differences in eye contact, attention span, and improved behavior without side effects. Concrete proof is yet to come, however.

Remember that unusual doses of any vitamin can react in the body much like medication, which must be monitored carefully. The body eliminates some unused vitamins but retains others, which can cause health problems. More information about vitamins is available from the Autism Research Institute.

Plan to Monitor Treatment

An important part of treatment is to identify a way to monitor medication for adverse effects. Your doctor will probably want a complete physical examination before starting the medication as a basis of comparison. The examination may include general laboratory tests of blood and urine. It should also include your observations. Report whether your child has any allergies or reactions to previous medications or is currently on medication for other problems, such as epilepsy or allergies.

Discuss the following before leaving the doctor's office with a prescription for your child:

Name of the medication: You may want to investigate on your own.

Results you expect from the medication.

Nontechnical explanation of how the medicine works.

Exact dose and how to administer it: Should the medication be taken with food, as with many strong drugs, or at a certain time of day?

Reactions to expect, positive and negative.

Interactions with other medicine or foods to avoid.

What to do if you miss a dose.

Availability of a less expensive generic form.

The doctor will probably start your child on the lowest dose and increase this if necessary. In emergencies, such as extreme self-destructiveness, your child may receive larger doses. As a behavior subsides, the dosages should gradually be reduced. Never stop a potent medicine abruptly, or your child may suffer withdrawal symptoms.

68

Be sure to involve teachers and therapists in your monitoring plan. Their observations under controlled situations can be invaluable. If you notice symptoms you never expected, contact the doctor immediately.

Medication therapy can help your child break through the communication barrier, but you and your child never learn who the real person is when drugs modify the picture. Long-term meaningful treatment comes from an approach grounded in consistent behavior management coupled with opportunities for your child to learn, communicate, and develop socially.

18

~~~~~~

HOW YOUNG CHILDREN DEVELOP

C hildren grow and learn every day. They mature through a continual process that combines their inborn abilities with information from the world around them. Each new accomplishment lays the groundwork for the next. Basic skills grow more complex with experience. This exciting process is *development*, and your child's skills and qualities unfold in this way, too.

Development follows a similar progression in all children. Each stage, however, includes a broad range of what is normal in terms of pace and sequence. One baby may walk at 12 months, another at 15 months. Some children skip stages or discover unusual patterns of advancing. They babble and connect words without first saying many single words. They scoot backward instead of crawling forward. These variations present clues about a child's particular learning style.

Your child's autism may alter this range of normal development. You probably have noticed some differences already. By studying the gradual process of ordinary development, you discover the wonders of your child's learning style. With this understanding comes a more realistic picture of what your child can accomplish.

Early Learning

Infants display the ability to learn, interact, and respond at birth. At first they focus on adapting to conditions outside the womb. Their immature nervous system, which controls all movements, responds to a satisfying environment. Babies listen for sounds and watch for sights they consider appealing. They accept comfort from parents who soothe them with gentle stroking, rocking, and quiet whispers and songs. The parent-child love affair begins.

As babies develop, their involuntary responses to sound, touch, and movement gradually become purposeful. Reflexes mature into muscles that attempt focused actions. Now youngsters seek out people and objects around them. They recognize facial expressions and voices and react with eye contact, coos, and smiles.

Parents who talk, play, and encourage their baby's explorations foster development. These interactions tell babies they are loved and accepted. Through these feelings, babies learn who they are and what influence they have on their world.

This growing self-awareness bolsters babies with the confidence to stretch themselves, to explore objects farther from their parents, and to learn about people beyond themselves and their caretakers. They become comfortable with their skills and emotions as separate from those of their parents. Their parents' love, acceptance, and support give them this independence.

Resources and professionals often talk about the developmental process in terms of five main categories besides physical growth: communication, cognition, sensorimotor, social and emotional, and self-help. You may hear these or similar terms in connection with your child.

Communication

Communication is one of a child's most remarkable achievements. The idea that a baby develops the facility to use words, symbols, or gestures to transmit information is astounding.

At first, communication is only a cry that helps babies gain control over their social environment. As time passes, infants cry less and produce more sounds. Babies learn to communicate by first observing language and then imitating what they see and hear. They practice vowel and consonant sounds representative of language around the world. When parents reinforce certain grunts and

71

coos, babies learn sounds typical of their native language. Slowly, these sounds turn into letters, words, and sentences.

Communication is transmitted by means of two pathways. *Receptive language* involves understanding words, symbols, and gestures. *Expressive language* is the ability to relate information through these same avenues. Most children understand more than they are able to communicate, although autism may interfere with this order for your child.

Cognition

Cognition refers to the fund of general information a child stores and processes. More specifically, cognitive skills include the ability to think, remember, reason, and solve problems. At first, babies use their senses of hearing, vision, smell, taste, and touch to gain understanding of their world. They respond according to their basic needs in very concrete ways.

As babies mature, they learn that objects exist even when they are out of sight. They understand more complicated concepts of cause and effect and how objects and people relate to each other. They interpret these perceptions and prior knowledge to solve everyday challenges. Without accurate perceptions, as in autism, the world becomes distorted and thinking impaired.

Sensorimotor Skills

Sensorimotor skills comprise large and small muscle movements and visual coordination of these actions. With *gross*, or large, *motor development*, children engage in body movements using large muscles. Head and trunk control develops first. As babies gain control of their bodies, they lift their heads and focus their eyes. Once babies focus, they can coordinate hand and eye movements and learn to sit, crawl, walk, and climb, all skills critical to exploring the world.

Large muscles mature before small muscles in the hands or feet. As *fine motor skills* in small muscles strengthen, babies gain the movements necessary for intricate hand and finger projects. They master poking, pointing, and squeezing.

These abilities lead to coordinated eye and hand movements necessary to pick up tiny objects. This skill is called *eye-hand coordination*, and it is important for learning to eat, dress, write, and take care of daily needs. Babies also explore their world with other senses of taste, smell, sound, and touch. These senses are critical to development. Through the senses, a child observes, imitates, and learns. Any problem in these areas contributes to misperceptions of the environment that can affect development.

Social and Emotional Skills

Social and emotional skills reflect a child's self-awareness and overall ability to interact with other children and adults. These skills are important to a child's total well-being.

A baby's first interactions are the give-and-take exchanges between parent and child. Children develop the basis for self-esteem from these early relationships. Initially, the baby demands instant gratification. As children mature, they develop patience. They pick up cues from interactions with others to develop the social skills of sharing, taking turns, and becoming friends. By understanding how to deal with people, children learn to function as members of a community. When children misperceive social messages, they are unable to act appropriately in social situations.

Self-help

With *self-help skills*, children learn to care for themselves. Infants completely depend on their caregivers. As they mature, babies assume greater responsibility for such activities of daily living as feeding, dressing, bathing, and toileting.

Table 2 reviews the average ages at which children accomplish certain developmental milestones. Remember, these are general guideposts to help you to understand better your child's development. Realize that isolated skills comprise only part of the total child. Each area intertwines with the others to form the core of your child's self-image. This is the main goal of raising any child— to help that little person feel good about herself and what she accomplishes.

Table 2
DEVELOPMENTAL MILESTONES

Activity	Averages for Nondisabled Children (Age in Months)
Lifts head	1.0–2
Smiles and coos	0.5–3
Rolls over	2.0–10
Focuses on objects	2.0–4
Holds objects	3.0–7
Interest in sounds	3.0–9
Sits independently	4.0–8
Rhythmic vocalizations	5.0–7
Crawls	6.0–11
Finger feeds	6.0–16
Says single words	7.0–14
Uses spoon	8.0–20
Walks	9.0–18
Solves simple problems	9.0–12
Says short sentences	13.0–30
Toilet self	18.0–48
Dresses	20.0–42

19

~~~~~~

DEVELOPMENT
WITH AUTISM

P arents usually take pride in watching their children grow and learn. They delight in nurturing someone who will walk, talk, and, later, live and work independently. You probably felt some of these joys during your child's infancy before you received a diagnosis of autism. With time, you will again find pleasure in your child's achievements, as most parents do.

Overall Progress

Your child's development may follow a distinctive course, just like that of other children. Complications arise, however, when factors associated with autism interfere with your youngster's ability to progress consistently. Your child may take longer to reach some milestones or seem locked into a given stage. An alarming aspect of autistic development is when a child progresses normally and then regresses to a younger stage or loses a skill entirely. The areas most affected are communication and social skills.

Try to stay hopeful. Concentrate on what your child *can* do, and build from there. By understanding autism and how it influences development, you can devise new strategies to overcome whatever challenges the disorder brings. For guidance in understanding some of your child's developmental stages, refer to the appendix "Developmental Symptoms of Autism."

Communication

An early symptom of autism is the failure to develop usable language. Babies with autism who coo and babble may have a smaller range of sounds than a child without autism, or they may squeal instead. The child who babbles during the first 8 months and says one or two words by 12 months may suddenly stop speaking. Because speech seems normal initially, parents and physicians wait for more. Sometimes another year or two passes before evaluation occurs.

By age two or three the problem becomes more obvious. At a time when other children know their name, respond to yes and no, understand abstract concepts of boy-girl, and follow simple commands, the child with autism may parrot what is said or lack speech completely. Instead of reaching, your child may move closer to what he wants and then scream, leaving you to figure out the dilemma.

As school age approaches, verbal communications may remain a major problem. Normal children understand language and use it to satisfy their needs. Children with autism, however, may lack the ability to comprehend and express themselves. Many have difficulty understanding any language taken out of context. Their language mimics what they hear in word, pitch, and tone, usually without meaning. Whereas nondisabled children usually understand more than they express, a child with autism may exhibit reverse skills or may seem to fluctuate in this ability.

Children with autism who develop language often sound mechanical in how they express words. Teachers sometimes first spot higher functioning children with autism at this time because their communications lack an understanding of abstract concepts.

Many professionals predict that children who are without usable language by age five have more limited futures. There is no magic cutoff, however. One educator reports a 6 year old who first gained language and went on to attain a college degree and live and work independently. Another tells of a child who was retarded but first spoke at 12 years and consequently acquired some social communication.

You can help your child with language by constantly talking about his activities and expanding his experiences. Consult Key 31, or talk with a trained speech pathologist for more specific suggestions to improve your child's communication skills.

Sensorimotor Skills

Autistic babies usually explore their surroundings by the senses of taste, smell, touch, and sound longer than normal infants and toddlers. Without adequate perceptions, these babies lack the ability to imitate and learn from their world. Consequently, they may miss important speech, social, and large and small motor skills. Unable to receive accurate messages from the environment, the baby with autism can be fussy, sometimes screaming for hours.

Within a year or two, many children with autism become captivated with stimulating their own bodies, even to the point of self-abuse. These children often show repetitive behaviors and fixate on lights or twinkling objects or move rhythmically to increase stimulation. Some children open and slam doors repeatedly, just for the sound or sight. They may spin their bodies or twirl objects for sensation rather than to explore the environment. Enjoyable interactions with adults may include roughhousing, such as tickling, tossing, or swirling the child to stimulate the senses.

Social and Emotional Skills

An infant with autism may miss cues from normal parent-child interactions. From the outset you may notice that your baby seems unable to respond to you the way he does to sights and sounds. He avoids eye contact or fusses unless you keep him in motion.

At six to eight months, he lacks the usual anxiety from approaching strangers or your leaving. By age two your child may withdraw from attempts to socialize in favor of self-stimulating behaviors, such as hand flapping or watching the laundry go around in the washing machine.

Although nondisabled children display a predictable range of emotions, your child's responses may seem unconnected to whatever and whoever he experiences. He laughs or screams without obvious reasons. He barely progresses beyond demanding instant gratification. If you interrupt self-play, he screams; if you are unable to understand his unusual communication attempts, he tantrums.

Social skills are one way to differentiate autism from mental retardation. Generally, a child who is retarded has social skills comparable to mental abilities. Although most children with autism demonstrate some affection by school age, their social skills usually lag behind mental ability.

By adolescence, tantrums and the need for strict routines lessen, although a small percentage of children continue with violent unprovoked tantrums. Even the most advanced teens remain aloof, and their affect appears flat. They have difficulty picking up cues about other people's feelings and participating in normal conversation. They may need to be taught each social skill that nondisabled teenagers acquire incidentally. With specific intervention techniques, however, your child can learn to respond socially.

Self-help

During normal development, most children gradually take charge of their own care. Your child may be delayed in obtaining self-help skills. Avoidance of any changes carries over to rejecting attempts to alter toileting, feeding, or dressing routines.

A child who would normally eat solid food at about six months may fight lumpy foods for years. Similarly, average toilet-training schedules of about three years may be pushed back until age four or five years in a child with autism. For some children, an inability to switch gears or secret fears play a role in sleep disturbances as well.

Children with autism can learn to care for themselves with targeted behavior modification programs. An important part of these programs is your patience in addressing independently each characteristic of autism.

Another aspect involves perseverance to challenge your youngster. Some parents of a child with disabilities fall into the trap of becoming overprotective or limiting change or responsibilities for fear of a blowup.

Whatever the reason, overprotectiveness interferes with development as much as any disability. Control your inclination to do everything for your child. Instead, monitor your child's growth as you would any child's. Provide opportunities to stimulate curiosity and promote maturation.

Try not to think of your youngster as autistic. Think of him as a human being who is your child. Work to modify his autistic characteristics, but work harder to strengthen the positive aspects of his development. Have faith that your child can develop further, and he will live up to this trust.

20

MENTAL ABILITIES

Historically, there have been two lines of thinking about mental ability and autism. One assumed that children who possessed high performance in isolated skills could perform equally well in all areas *if they chose*. This view presumed that autism was a psychological problem and children could control their autistic symptoms, which is untrue.

The other assumption referred to the multitudes of people with autism who were in inferior programs or who lived in institutions. Staff undervalued the capabilities of anyone who functioned below average. Old-line institutions offered few educational or social opportunities to stimulate intellectual growth. Severe behaviors that could have been reduced were either stifled by overmedication or allowed to persist, interfering with learning. Without motivation, people who had autism lived up to the low expectations set for them.

Nowadays, most children with autism live at home. Their parents furnish loving homes and advocate for early intervention programs, improved special education, and increased social acceptance. With quality support, your child's potential for learning is limitless.

Measuring Intelligence
Your baby's progress may be measured against developmental scales. Much of the information to complete these scales comes from observation sessions and parent interviews. *Developmental scales* compare your child's milestones, such as crawling and babbling, with norms for a given age.

When autism is suspected, the evaluator may correlate these skills with a specific scale for autistic behaviors, such as the

American Psychiatric Association diagnostic criteria (See Key 2). Overall scale scores offer some idea of how your baby's development compares with that of others of the same age or with that of other children who have autism. They cannot predict how much your baby will learn, however.

Schools measure intelligence by *standardized tests*, which assess how your child applies thinking and performance to information acquired from formal and informal learning. An *intelligence quotient*, or *IQ*, is calculated from the test scores and then compared with scores from other people of the same age. The results determine your child's general mental age. Keep in mind that mental age refers only to the composite intelligence test score: it does not consider a person's experience or functioning.

When Autism Includes Mental Retardation

A diagnosis of *mental retardation* indicates that a child processes information more slowly than other people the same age: *learning definitely takes place, but at a reduced rate*. The slower the rate, the more difficulty a child has with reasoning, evaluating, remembering, and associating ideas. Language and social skills usually mature at a rate similar to intellectual abilities.

In autism, social and language skills typically lag behind overall cognitive development. A child may be able to read but understand little of what is read or may master basic academic subjects but be unable to hold a conversation.

Studies vary in reporting the percentage of mental retardation in children with autism, although the Society of Autism notes that 70 percent have some form of mental retardation. Generally, higher functioning children tend to come out better on standardized tests and to exhibit less extreme social withdrawal and speech difficulties.

Some recent research claims that this IQ remains constant throughout life, thereby forecasting future intelligence. O. Ivar Lovaas, however, a leader in behavior modification, found an average increase of 20 IQ points and major education gains for children involved in intensive behavior management programs.

81

Whether or not mental retardation accompanies autism, your child will benefit from the same structured treatment geared to individual differences. For now, forget the timetable applied to other children. Your child's progress may take longer, but you will see gains.

Elimination of Strict IQ Classifications

Recently, the American Association of Mental Retardation deemphasized the importance of IQ in establishing mental retardation. The organization revised its previous definition to eliminate old labels of mild, moderate, severe, and profound. The new definition regards intellectual functioning below a 70 to 75 IQ but recognizes significant limitations in two or more adaptive skill areas, such as self-care and social skills. It also maintains that the condition must exist from childhood (age 18 or under). With this definition, how a child acts is more important than a test score for overall adjustment.

Extraordinary Skills

One fascination of autism involves isolated outstanding, or *savant*, skills. A savant child shows uncharacteristic talent in one area, sometimes way above average. For example, a child can test as moderately mentally retarded but play the piano with perfect pitch or memorize telephone book pages at a glance.

The most common savant skills are drawing, calendar calculation, writing, rote memory, music, and advanced reading. Leo Kanner called these puzzling abilities *islets of intelligence* when he first differentiated the characteristics of autism. Although 50 percent of savants have autism, only about 10 percent of children with autism have outstanding skills.

The cause for these unusual talents is unknown. Still, parents should encourage this ability. Some children tend to lose their savant skill as symptoms of autism decrease. Other high-functioning individuals have expanded their narrow interests into careers as adults. Most savants to date, however, never find functional avenues for their splinter skills.

Pros and Cons of Testing Mental Development

Mental growth in children with autism is difficult to assess. These children, particularly at younger ages, often refuse to cooperate in testing situations. Even when they sit still, intelligence tests have been known to contradict each other, and developmental scale results have been criticized because they often rely on parent or teacher observations.

Still, you can find many professionals who rely on intelligence tests as predictors of educational and social outcome. They claim that intelligence testing is valid and that the results remain consistent over time.

Too much trust in testing, however, overlooks the whole battery of skills necessary to function in real-life situations. A child who scores higher on formalized tests but is without social skills may adapt poorly within the community, whereas someone who tests lower but volunteers language and can take care of daily needs has a greater potential for independent living.

Another complication of autism is the difference between scores on verbal and nonverbal portions of tests. By one estimate, about 25 percent of children with autism score normally on performance batteries and low on verbal tasks. Another 25 percent achieve normal language and performance scores, and 50 percent test in the retarded range in both areas.

Anyone dealing with a single composite score misses the strengths and weaknesses with each area. A truer assessment of mental ability is more in quality of life than an IQ score.

21

HELPING YOUR YOUNG CHILD PROGRESS

Every day is a challenge with any child. Your child's disability may add erratic behavior, extra therapy sessions, and formalized home exercises that can strain the most composed family, both mentally and physically. Here are some recommendations to reduce the pressures of taking care of your child with autism while encouraging her progress.

Identify Reachable Goals

Take a realistic assessment of your child now. Think about what you would like the next step to be. Expectations give you and your family something to work toward. They provide the automatic structure to persevere when you feel overextended or discouraged.

Be flexible enough to reevaluate goals as your child changes, which will happen. Use the goals as guideposts rather than limitations. Goals that are unrealistic or too high or low can frustrate you and your child.

Motivate your youngster by deciding goals together, once she is able to communicate with you. Reachable goals give you hope and your child self-confidence.

Foster Independence

Even the youngest child should be expected to assume responsibility for her actions. Autism is no excuse for not learning to contribute to the family, but autism may mean you need to plan consciously for learning those household tasks most families take for granted.

- Clear your child's bedroom of anything that can be harmful. Make the room a safe haven for bedtime, play, and rest periods, so you can concentrate on other responsibilities worry free.
- Move toys and clothing into drawers and shelves your child can reach. Make a few favorites accessible, and store the rest in a safe place, if your child is destructive. Rotate your child's choices.
- Install a low hook in the coat closet so your child can reach and hang outerwear. Similarly, lower clothes bars in your child's closet.
- Make sure clothes and shoes fit properly and can be fastened easily. If your child has difficulty with buttons and snaps, insert Velcro tabs.
- Develop a daily routine of washing, hair care, toothbrushing, and dressing that reinforces good grooming and independent dressing. Give your child a hairstyle that is easy to manage.
- Offer your child choices. Learning to choose teaches a child how to make decisions. Any child can decide daily life issues, such as clothing options, preferred activities, or which chores to complete first. As your child matures, offer higher level decision-making responsibilities, such as selecting, buying, and preparing weekly lunches. Oversee clothing choices so that the items go together and suit the activity and weather. If color matching is a concern, buy all clothes in the same favorite two or three coordinating colors.
- Leave a stool in the bathroom for your child to reach the sink and her necessary toiletries.
- Organize a specific place for your child's possessions. Make sure she learns to replace them after each usage or at the close of each day, whichever is the house rule. Begin cleanup habits early. They may take a long time to become automatic.
- Set a timer for how long your child should take for an activity. If she complains, tell her that the clock sets the rules, not you.

Mastery of self-care activities allows your child to feel good about herself and eventually relieve you of part of the responsibility. Even if your child resists some of these activities at first, work toward a goal of independent grooming.

Structure Positive Sessions Together

Realize that you are your child's first and most important teacher. Your talking and interacting play a key role in how she develops. Even if your child seems aloof, she thrives on your hugs, roughhousing, and soothing voice.

Every source you consult reinforces how your care and persistence will give your child the confidence to learn. This news can be a heavy burden, however. Don't allow teaching your child to become a full-time job. You have a home, family, and perhaps outside work to balance. Structure your child's environment to provide her with the stimulation she needs while allowing you freedom to attend to other responsibilities.

- Decorate walls in your child's room with items that interest her, such as family photographs. Pictures reinforce learning and language without your interaction. Allow your child to be attracted to what you want her to learn.
- Plan activity times for when you and your child are both rested. Consider which time of day your child is most alert and you have the fewest distractions. Weary, tense people cannot enjoy themselves, let alone hold productive sessions. Similarly, end a session or switch activities if you or your child becomes uneasy or tired. Learn both your limits. Divide activity times into shorter periods throughout the day instead of exhausting yourselves with one session. At times your child may be hard to engage, which may be frustrating, but don't give up. Being alone is not a rational decision for children with autism. Conserve your energy by not feeling compelled to stimulate your child every free moment.
- Learn your child's distinctive signals. All children, even nonverbal children, convey messages about how they feel. Maybe your child flaps her hands more vigorously when she's upset or has a special cry for hunger. These clues allow you to redirect activities before behavior problems occur. By recognizing simple attempts at communication, you give your child the confidence to reach out further.
- Imitate your child. Autism may disrupt your child's natural ability to duplicate others. Yet, imitation is the main way youngsters

learn. Break into your child's world by mimicking the sounds and movements she produces. Once you have her attention, she may imitate you in return.

- Extend your child's fascination. If your child has an extreme interest, transform it into a socially acceptable activity. For example, one child walked in circles and talked to herself. These discussions were a way to hear about what went on during the day. They also became bedtime stories for a younger brother.

- Be ready to repeat activities. You may need several sessions to sustain your child's attention enough for her to learn. Repetition increases the likelihood that learning will take place and helps your child feel comfortable with a concept or activity. You may find repetition is boring. Resist the temptation to change activities unless your child gives you cues that the time is right.

- Vary your child's activities. At home, encourage your child to experience different sights, smells, sounds, and textures. Reinforce this learning on outings and walks to stores, playgrounds, or museums. Children with autism may have difficulty generalizing what they learn to new situations. These outings can extend learning and be part of your regular errands. To avert problems with changing environments, talk with your child about what to expect for the day. Review what will happen next and for how long so your child feels more comfortable. Describe what you see during your travels.

- Admit that sometimes you don't feel like teaching your child. Take a break. Don't feel guilty that you need time to renew yourself. Every parent does.

- Be positive about teaching your child. The idea is to make learning into fun games and social experiences. Stimulating your child is supposed to be enjoyable, not a burden.

Keep a diary of your child's successes. Periodically, review her progress and celebrate her achievements, no matter how modest. Help your child develop a positive sense of herself through these accomplishments. Make time to relax, learn, and have fun together.

22

~~~~~~

BEHAVIOR MANAGEMENT

B ehavior often poses the greatest challenge to raising a child with autism. Odd repetitive movements, unpredictability, and disorderly outbursts may defeat and isolate you more than any other aspect of the disability.

At home, your child's behavior can drain your energy. In social situations, you may feel others are judging your parenting of an unruly child who otherwise looks normal. Don't allow your child's behavior to keep you from being a family. There are alternatives.

Begin by Setting Rules

Every child craves discipline, and so does your child. Set well-defined rules, and establish what happens should these rules be broken. Make sure rules and routines are fair for everyone. Do they fit the situation? Can your other children live with rules adapted for someone with autism? Equally important, are the rules understandable enough for your child's level of functioning?

Some parents resist disciplining the child with autism. They feel sorry for the youngster or harbor guilt about the disability. If the child is retarded, they believe this is all the more reason he cannot learn to behave. Other parents view discipline as punishment rather than guidelines for happy, healthy development. Your child needs discipline to feel secure within his world just as you need guidelines to run your home or place of employment.

Be Consistent

Many children with autism have difficulty picking up cues from their environment. They may learn a behavior but cannot

88

adapt, or generalize, it to new people, places, or situations. Arranging conditions so they are predictable helps children practice how to respond appropriately. When family members react with the same words or actions, a child interprets these as cues for repeating certain behaviors. Once a child learns appropriate behavior, be sure to arrange similar but varying situations to practice the behavior until it becomes automatic.

Family members who are inconsistent give your child the message that the unacceptable is eventually allowed if the troublesome behavior continues long enough. For example, a parent sometimes picks up a child who cries for attention instead of consistently waiting until the child stops crying and then holds the child as a reward. The single most important thing you can do to help your child behave is to be consistent.

Use Positive Reinforcement to Modify Behavior

Children with autism are often unsure about how to act. Like all children, however, they repeat behaviors that make them feel good. A subtle way to guide your child's learning is to praise, or reward, behaviors you want repeated. Your positive reaction gives him confidence. This satisfaction increases the likelihood that he will behave the same way again. Psychologists call this approval *positive reinforcement*. Focusing on the positive helps you see how well your child can act and how competent your child-rearing skills really are.

The most effective method to date for changing autistic actions is *behavior modification*. Behavior modification offers an orderly plan for molding how your child acts. The system uses rewards, or positive reinforcement, to strengthen what is acceptable and punishment, or aversives, to discourage the unacceptable.

A guiding principle behind behavior modification is that every behavior has a consequence. Whether the consequence is rewarding or negative determines whether someone wants to repeat the same behavior. Just as rewards presented consistently after a specific behavior tend to increase that behavior's recurrence, consistent punishments, such as verbal reprimands, usually lead to a decrease in the behavior.

There are many interpretations and technical terms for behavior modification, but the basic principles are similar. Consult with your child's teacher or therapist to coordinate efforts to modify your child's behavior. Otherwise, use your common sense to apply behavior modification when retraining your child's behavior. Here are some guidelines to follow:

- *Identify behaviors you want to change.* Choose only one or two concerns to deal with at a time. Perhaps you want to reduce a stereotyped behavior or teach your child to sit at the dinner table for 15 minutes. Limiting which behaviors to work on helps you to be more consistent and gives your child a greater opportunity to succeed without becoming confused or overloaded.

- *Document when and how often the behavior occurs.* From this observation, you may be able to analyze what triggers your child's behavior or find patterns in the way he acts. For example, you may find that changing the environment, such as moving chairs away from the table your child climbs on, redirects your child's behavior in a positive way.

- *Select a positive reinforcer, or reward, that motivates your child.* This can be tricky with autism. Your child may need more than a smile, happy voice, or hug to work for initially. Consider a rubdown, roughhousing, or more tangible rewards of nonsugared cereal or inexpensive toys. Some children can tell you what they want. Older children may enjoy coins and stickers to collect and exchange for baseball cards or release from unpleasant chores. Remember that the goal is to phase out tangible rewards in favor of more social rewards, such as verbal praise. With time, your child will behave in an acceptable way because it feels good.

- *Determine a schedule for presenting rewards.* You can reward your child immediately after completing a task, every hour, or at bedtime. The timing depends upon your child's ability to connect the reward with the correct behavior. Reward your child more often if he is unable to comprehend what you want. At first, provide a reward each time your child performs the desired behavior or at frequent intervals while the behavior keeps occurring. Verbally praise your child at the same time. You want him to

90

understand which behavior deserves the reward. For example, say, Good sitting still. Be sure to remind your child what *is* acceptable to do so he doesn't replace one unacceptable behavior with another.

• *Prepare a chart to document the number of times your child receives rewards for a specific behavior.* A chart allows your child to follow his progress and you to evaluate whether the plan is working. Initially, undesirable behaviors may increase. This is your child's way of testing and learning the rules. Within a couple of weeks, the behavior should decrease. Gradually lengthen intervals between each time you reward your child, and switch from tangible rewards to hugs and verbal praise.

If your child's behavior persists, you may need to alter one of these conditions:

1. Change the reward to something that motivates him better.
2. Shorten the intervals between rewards so you can catch your child doing the right thing more frequently.
3. Reevaluate whether what you are working to reduce is the correct behavior.

As your child progresses, you can use a chart to monitor responsibilities. (See Table 3.) Each day, go through a list with your child at predetermined times. Place a star, X, or fun sticker in the box for every completed activity. Review your child's progress, and add responsibilities as he can handle them. A chart adds structure to the day without your overinvolvement.

Behavior modification offers a nonthreatening, nonemotional, and organized approach to handling your child at a time when you may be close to your limit emotionally. The method is one of many tools to help your child and family refocus and stay on a positive path.

Overlook Attention-Getting Behavior

Ignoring is another technique to eliminate attention-getting behavior. By ignoring a behavior you take away the reward, which is your attention. Refuse any eye contact, touching, or words every

Table 3
SAMPLE CHART

MY JOBS

Jobs	Mon	Tues	Wed	Thurs	Fri	Sat	Sun
Turn off alarm							
Wash face and hands							
Brush teeth							
Comb hair							
Fold pajamas							
Dress							
Make bed							

time your child engages in the behavior you want eliminated, such as tantrums or screams. At first, the behavior may escalate to test your determination. Eventually, the behavior will end. When behavior is difficult to ignore, find something to keep yourself occupied. Otherwise, leave the room.

Time-out

Some behaviors are so disturbing they are impossible to ignore. You may need to hold your child to calm him or keep him safe. Another tactic is *time-out*. With time-out, you calmly remove your child from the situation and place him in another room or in a chair or other designated time-out place. Time-out gives you respite and provides your child a chance to calm down.

Set a timer to signal the length of time-out, or tell your child he can return after the negative behavior stops. This way, either the clock or your child controls your child's behavior. Make sure you verbalize why your child is in time-out, and recommend an appropriate behavior as replacement.

Be assured that your child wants to learn acceptable behavior, and you have the right to expect it. When you help your child manage behavior, you are really offering a fairer, more loving way to live.

23

‸‸

TREATMENTS AND TRENDS

T he unresolved mysteries of autism attract considerable interest, researchers, and offbeat treatments. This means that you
as a parent have more information to sort through in trying to
determine the right course for your child.

Avoiding Trends

Understand that children with autism display a broad spectrum of characteristics, many that change throughout development. One program cannot serve every child's needs. What helps
one child may be useless for your child. Evaluate a treatment program in light of your child's individual symptoms, strengths, and
weaknesses. Be cautious about any program that claims to *cure*
your child. Here are some factors to consider before permitting
your child to follow a new treatment plan:

- Remember that the only treatment plan to survive the test of time
  and lasting benefits is a *structured* (predictable, not rigid) *educational program that manages behavior through behavior modification and targets goals to individual levels of functioning.*
  Even if your child experiences a breakthrough with a particular
  technique, this must be supported by an educational program that
  offers the skills necessary for a fulfilling life within the community, including employment, recreation, and daily living skills.
- Investigate program claims before committing your child and
  family to a given plan. Ask the following questions:

    What is involved in treatment?
    Can treatment harm my child?

Is the treatment based on proven studies?

Does treatment interfere with my child's educational
goals? How will the two be integrated?

What will treatment mean for my family?

Will treatment be excessively costly and hook our family into
many months of sessions without giving us the tools to
reinforce and carry over gains?

Does this program address my child's individual needs, or are
all participants treated alike?

Has my child been properly evaluated for this plan?

How will my child be monitored?

- Discuss program options with an objective professional or
another parent who knows your child and who has nothing to
gain from your child participating in the program.
- Try to leave emotion out of your decision. At a time when you
may be vulnerable, some people will try to convince you that
their treatment is your child's only hope. Nothing could be further from the truth. With more investigation, you will learn that
there are always other options. Be realistic about your child, but
never give up hope.

Alternative Treatment Review

Throughout this book you will read many suggestions for
dealing with autism. Different sections cover education programs,
medications, diet, and behavior modification. As you search elsewhere, you may hear about other programs that allege beneficial
results. Some work on isolated symptoms; others are merely new
names for older ideas or offshoots of earlier philosophies. In certain instances, therapies have become quite controversial. These
are the most publicized alternatives. Check the resources to locate
more in-depth information about these options.

Sensory Integration

During the 1960s, Dr. Jean Ayres at the University of
California discovered that children with brain disorders were
unable to respond to incoming sensations in a functional manner.
She proposed therapeutic activities that tap a child's natural ability

94

to stimulate the normal activity of the damaged senses. The Ayres program provides play exercises to activate *proprioception,* input from the brain to muscles and joints, and the *vestibular sense,* how the body moves through space and changes head position, in addition to touch, sight, and hearing.

Only trained physical or occupational therapists administer sensory integration therapy. Occupational therapists, who are health professionals normally concerned with occupational performance, concentrate on play and learning as the work of children. Rather than a total program, sensory integration can relieve specific sensory-related symptoms of autism. Sensory Integration International sends information and maintains a list of qualified therapists.

Auditory Integration Training

Many people with autism experience intense sensitivity to sound that distorts what they hear. These sounds can be so painful that children develop behaviors, such as dazed rocking, to block them. Auditory training first establishes unusual hearing with an audiometric test. The following series of treatment sessions involves playing recorded sounds that filter out the painful frequencies so a child is able to hear other frequencies.

Treatment essentially retrains the sense of hearing by desensitizing the ear to certain unpleasant sounds. Some parents claim auditory integration training reduces some odd sounds and behaviors associated with their child's sound sensitivity. Research is still being conducted.

Visual Therapy

Scotopic sensitivity syndrome is a perceptual dysfunction caused by light sensitivity, which can result in visual distortions that can impede social awareness, self-esteem, and information processing. Helen Irlen developed Irlen Filters, colored filters or overlays that are added to glasses, as a form of visual therapy. Irlen believes that the filters modify problem light waves for users.

Irlen Filters are used worldwide. Although their benefits are still being researched, they gained popularity when author Donna

Williams participated in a media tour for her latest book on autism. The filters will not suddenly teach reading or other skills; however, some reports claim that the correct blend of colors in a filter aids integration of the senses and improves attention to visual stimuli. (Consult the resources in the appendix for more information.)

Options Institute

The Options approach is a labor-intensive and intrusive program based on the idea of unconditional acceptance of a child's behavior. It developed after professionals told a former advertising executive and his wife, Barry and Samahria Kaufman, that their 18-month-old son with autism required institutionalization. Barry wrote about his son's progress in *Son-Rise* and *A Miracle to Believe In* and began teaching other parents to treat their children at home.

A big problem with Options is that the program suggests psychological causes for autism that can be alleviated with love. *Constant attention to any child is likely to bring some changes.* With Options, medical professionals claim that the greatest changes come from positive parent attitudes rather than lessening the autism. Another concern is the Kaufmans' refusal to submit to independent evaluation. They say evaluation would distort the program's nonjudgmental philosophy.

Aversive Therapy

Aversive therapy, or negative reinforcement, is usually a last resort for a few families to prevent extreme self-abuse or destructive behavior. Use of aversives, such as cattle prods, shock, or other forms of physical punishment, has been the cause of law suits and considerable controversy.

Advocates claim aversive therapy offers a window of opportunity to teach damaged and unresponsive children. Any pain resulting from therapy can be minimal compared with what these children cause themselves. Opponents say the children are unable to say how great their pain is. They wonder how you can teach children that it is wrong to be violent if you are violent with them. Read Key 22 to discover more positive ways to handle your child's behavior: They work, even with the most self-abusive child.

Facilitated Communication

This relatively new and controversial method formalizes earlier attempts to help children with disabilities communicate with computers. With facilitated communication, a facilitator, or trained professional, guides a person's wrist as he or she types letters into a computer keyboard, enabling the child to communicate. Ideally, the facilitator reduces support until prompting is only a touch on the shoulder. Programs that use facilitated communication claim that people who were once believed incapable of logical thought are beginning to communicate.

Opponents worry that children who already talk or use sign language may give it up in favor of the attention from facilitated communication. They question the surprisingly high level of communications some of these children type. They warn that some children have difficulty switching facilitators, which makes critics wonder who is really moving the child's hand, the child or the facilitator.

Advocates argue that students make their own consistent typographical and spelling errors regardless of who facilitates for them. They contend that students often respond and answer questions in areas in which the facilitator had no prior knowledge. Facilitated communication can be helpful as another tool for breaking into a child's world. It cannot replace ordinary real-world communication, however, which is through speech.

Investigate credible approaches you think might help your child. Allow time for the method to work. Most important, monitor your child's progress and halt any program that interferes with your child's chances of performing independently in the community.

24

^^^

YOUR CHILD'S LEGAL RIGHT TO EDUCATION

C onsistent, relevant education is critical to your child's progress. Yet, every day a school district somewhere denies a child with autism the right to education. How does this happen? Parents are unaware of their rights to advocate on their child's behalf. Even when families understand their legal options, they must work around long waiting lists, funding and program shortages, and outdated attitudes.

An important step toward promoting your child's education is knowing current laws and their jargon. Newly expanded laws that are updated regularly guarantee your child's rights to greater educational opportunities and a more productive future.

Rehabilitation Act of 1973 (Public Law 93-112)
and Americans with Disabilities Act of 1990
(Public Law 101-336)

The Rehabilitation Act of 1973 was the first public statement restricting discrimination against people with disabilities. Section 504 of the act specifically ensures your child's equal access to any school receiving public funds. The federal government withholds money from education, vocational, and adult education programs or places of employment that obstruct opportunities because of your child's disability.

The Americans with Disabilities Act of 1990 strengthens the Rehabilitation Act by guaranteeing equal access to employment, public accommodation, transportation, state and local government services, and telecommunications for anyone with a disability. Even though these laws have been in effect for some time, the implications for your child are still open to interpretation at the local level. If you need more information or want to file a complaint, contact the U.S. Department of Justice, Civil Rights Division.

Education for Handicapped Children Act (Public Law 94-142)

Every school-age child has the right to free public education. In 1975, Congress passed Public Law 94-142 to guarantee the same right for the child with autism. With this legislation and its amendments, the federal government provided the framework for the following government-funded special education programs by setting these requirements:

Schools must provide free appropriate public education to everyone between 3 and 21 years. "Appropriate" refers to a learning situation that suits your child's needs and at public expense, whether in a public or private setting. Moreover, your child has the right to a curriculum that is functional for future adaptation to community living.

Education for children with disabilities in the *least restrictive environment*, that is, a setting most integrated with non-handicapped children. Services may be offered in separate classes or school *only* when your child's disability prevents satisfactory achievement within a regular education placement. In regions with too few children with disabilities, several school districts may join together to support a cooperative special education district. Severe disability may require a more specialized setting, perhaps outside the district.

Students must receive an evaluation of specific needs before involvement in any special education services. Testing should be nondiscriminatory, and testers must adjust for any factors, such as hearing loss, that influence outcome. If your family speaks a language besides English at home, you can request that an interpreter accompany your child through testing or that your child be tested by a professional who speaks your language. These services are at the school district's expense.

99

Students must receive the additional recommended services that are necessary for learning, such as speech, occupational or physical therapy, transportation, and counseling.

Children who are eligible for special education must receive services based on a written individualized education program (IEP) for school-age students or an individualized family service plan (IFSP) for infants and toddlers. These plans state the type of special education, related services, and goals for various areas of development that relate to your child. (See Key 27.)

Individualized plans must be reviewed regularly and changed to adapt to your child's progress. This is especially important with autism because your child may progress enough that symptoms become more characteristic of another disability, such as learning disability or retardation, which may influence program choices. A formal review meeting takes place annually, and full reevaluation must be conducted every three years.

The law guarantees the rights of children with disabilities and their guardians by ensuring their participation in the planning process. Therefore, you can challenge any part of your child's plan you find incompatible with your child's goals.

The Education for Handicapped Children Act established standards for allocating services to children with disabilities. Yet, it upheld state practices that excluded children from indispensable support because they were age three to five or had reached a given cutoff age.

Education of the Handicapped Amendment of 1986 (Public Law 99-457)

The abundance of literature confirming the benefits of special education for very young children contributed to the passage of Public Law 99-457 in 1986. This amendment established incentives for states to serve all children from ages three to five with disabilities. It also made funds available to states that developed programs to serve children from birth through two years who were at risk of developing disabilities. As a result, several states created child-find programs to locate children with developmental delays.

Individuals with Disabilities Education Act (IDEA) (Public Law 101-476)

This 1990 amendment to the Education for Handicapped Act expanded and clarified critical services for children and youth with disabilities. Autism became a separate category, which means your child is entitled to appropriate programming and placement by staff trained in autism. In addition, the new law required states to establish programs for children aged three to five and to investigate alternatives for those younger than three.

The amendment also mandated government payment for assistive devices, such as hearing aids or voice amplifiers, for anyone who needed them to learn. For older youths with disabilities, IDEA guaranteed a process for the transition from school to adult community programming. School personnel are to investigate plans for future education or employment, housing, recreation, and general community adjustment by a student's sixteenth birthday.

The laws give each state considerable license for interpretation. Unfortunately, individual clarification translates into program gaps that may leave out your child, especially if he or she is disruptive.

To identify services in your district, contact the local school district, state education department, child-find office, or local parent organization (Autism Society of America). For written information about national legislation and your child's rights, contact the National Information Center for Children and Youth with Disabilities or the Family Resource Center on Disabilities, which coordinates Parent and Information Centers nationwide.

101

25

PARENT RIGHTS

N ot long ago, professional wisdom dictated that parents of children with autism be excluded from their child's education. Thankfully, this era is over. Current laws grant specific rights and responsibilities to parents, including those having a child with autism, during the special education process. Legislation entitles your involvement in decisions concerning your child's evaluation, placement, and educational program.

Right to Consent

Local school districts require your permission to conduct any developmental, neurological, speech and hearing, psychological, or educational assessment. After testing, your consent is essential to prepare and finalize plans tailored to your child's needs. *Consent* means you fully understand any information relevant to whatever activity your child's team discusses at a planning meeting.

Although a signature is optional, your agreement to initial placement and future changes is necessary. Most school districts request a signature on an individualized education program as evidence of your approval of the recommended plan. Copies of signed documents are important for your files, too.

Responsibility to Participate

Before your child can receive special education services of any kind, the local school district must prepare an individualized education program (IEP). According to law, you have a clearly defined role in drafting and monitoring your child's IEP.

Notification

The local school district must inform you of any meetings to develop, review, or revise your child's IEP and take steps to schedule hearings at a time and place that are agreeable to everyone. You

102

must receive notice in enough time to ensure that one or both of you can attend. Your meeting notice must state the purpose, time, location, and names and titles of participants. If you communicate in a language other than English, either bring along or request an interpreter.

Participation

The law expects you to participate as an equal during planning meetings. Listen to what school personnel discovered about your child. Share your education concerns and goals. Discuss together your child's need for special education and related services. Decide with other participants the best school services for your child.

Use the opportunity to clarify procedures. Ask participants to explain any test, terms, or labels you do not understand completely. Your child may have skill peaks and valleys that defy easy program answers or may perform poorly on language-based tests. Make sure recommendations rely on more than test results.

You have the right to bring an advocate to meetings. Advocates can be supportive friends or neighbors, your child's independent evaluator, or trained advocates from a local government agency or parent organization, such as The Association for Persons with Severe Handicaps, the Autism Society of America, or the Family Resource Center on Disabilities.

Inability to Attend

When you are unable to attend, the district must determine another method to secure your participation, such as by individual or conference call or facsimile. A meeting can be conducted without you only if the district shows good faith in trying to reach you. District personnel must keep detailed records of telephone calls or letters indicating these attempts. In the event of your absence, you receive a written summary of the meeting for approval. Make every effort to go, however. *These meetings are important for you to attend.*

Right to Disagree

You have the right to challenge any suggestions regarding your child's diagnosis, evaluation, services, and placement. It is hoped that you and the district can resolve differences without outside mediation.

Perhaps a trial period may work as a compromise. You and the district agree to test a proposal and assess your child's progress after a given time period. You may want to talk with school personnel informally or write a letter about your concerns. You can also exercise the option to request another IEP meeting. If you question only one aspect of the IEP, the rest of the plan can still be implemented while you settle the problem.

If you and the district cannot resolve your differences or if they refuse your repeated requests to meet, the law mandates an appeals process you can pursue on your child's behalf. Each state provides procedures called due process, for appealing a decision. Under *due process*, you agree to meet with school representatives and an impartial hearing officer appointed by the state. The officer hears both opinions and drafts an independent decision.

Agreeing to talk with a mediator does not eliminate your right to state-level review. If you disagree with the mediator's decision, you can still seek legal action. The Handicapped Children's Protection Act of 1986 (Public Law 99-372) entitles you to an attorney without charge to represent you in state or federal court.

Due process can be very time consuming and complicated, depending upon the state. During the process, your child will continue with the last agreed-upon IEP, unless you and the education team agree otherwise. Check with your state department of education for guidelines concerning appeals and requests for due process hearings.

Right of Confidentiality

School districts maintain individual files on each student. Records of academic performance, health, and behavior, test results, and communications regarding IEP meetings are part of typical files.

You have the right to review the file, challenge its contents, and guard access to and release of information about your child. The law provides the following safeguards to your child's privacy:

> You and your child, when qualified, can review educational records and copy them for your own files. Copies are important when your child attends other programs or moves to the next level of schooling. Many school districts keep records for only a brief time after a student leaves.

> You have the right to seek explanations and interpretations of records from school officials.

> School officials must keep records as long as there is an outstanding request to review them.

> You can request corrections in records you find inaccurate, misleading, or an invasion of your child's rights. Should school officials refuse, they must reply in writing so you can request a due process hearing.

> Schools must keep track of requests for records from other education and social service agencies that are authorized to examine student files. Your child's file should show verification of these requests.

Responsibility to Become Involved

Parent involvement has been recognized as so critical to education that states hold training sessions to familiarize parents with the laws. These laws keep changing, however. The past three decades have seen sweeping legal changes in favor of individuals with disabilities.

Still, some districts are consolidating services because of budget crunches and the federal government is considering limiting attorney fee reimbursement, so you must stay current. Contact your state parent information and training project through the office of special education, the Family Resource Center on Disabilities, or the Autistic Society of America for details about sessions available near you. Take advantage of your rights by staying informed.

26

SCHOOL ASSESSMENT

E ven if your child has a confirmed diagnosis, you still need to follow a similar evaluation process for qualification in school district early intervention and special education programs. Evaluation is the first step toward assuring appropriate education for your child. It involves gathering information about your child's total development and assessing the outcomes to answer these questions:

Does your child have a disability that interferes with
learning?
Is the disability severe enough to warrant assistance for your
child to progress? If so, which services?

An initial request for evaluation may come from you, your physician, the school, or your child's teacher. With each situation, your written permission is necessary before assessment can begin. By law, states *must* evaluate, at no fee to parents, children suspected of needing special education by age three. More states now finance child-find programs that identify younger children who are at risk of having a disability.

Try to contact your local school principal or director of special education to apply for assessment as soon as you have concerns. Should you find that your district lacks infant evaluation, ask the principal to refer you to another university or medical or social service agency that can assess your baby's learning.

If the school denies your preschooler or school-age child an evaluation, obtain an explanation for the refusal in writing. Keep a copy of the letter in case you disagree and decide to appeal the decision to the state office of special education. Many school districts are unfamiliar with autism and how to incorporate such a child into their system, so they refuse to try. The law rejects this argument. You may want to contact The Association for Persons with Severe Handicaps, the Family Resource Center on Disabilities, or the Autism Society of America for an advocate to help you acquire services for your child.

Although the appraisal process is similar across the United States, each state sets its own procedures. Your child may encounter any combination of case manager or social worker, school psychologist, speech and language pathologist, physical or occupational therapist, educational specialist, and classroom teacher. These individuals, plus you, comprise the multidisciplinary team assessing your child's functional performance.

Expect your child to be tested and observed by several people. Federal law dictates that special education placement be based on the results of more than a single test. Consequently, evaluators may examine the same problem with more than one test or may require several visits for an accurate appraisal of performance.

The choice of assessment tools is left to each evaluator. The only requirement is that tests be nondiscriminatory, conducted in your primary spoken language, and suitable for your child. To learn more about the most frequently given test, see Suggested Reading.

A *case manager* is your liaison with the education team. This person is responsible for coordinating information needed by the team to make responsible decisions. The case manager will request medical records and reports or tests from other professionals who examined your youngster.

The team will also want to know your observations. Your child may perform some tasks in one situation but not in another, such as testing. Some unusual talents may never be uncovered within the confines of formal testing protocol. These variations are important for you to share.

Very young and nonverbal children may be evaluated with developmental scales that measure a child's performance against standardized age norms. The scales draw upon how your child behaves at home. Accordingly, your input is essential to the assessment process.

School districts usually have their own evaluation team to conduct testing at the local school or district office. Some districts, however, contract specific services outside the system to private individual or agency evaluators. Your child's case manager should arrange any outside assessment without cost to you.

Whoever evaluates your child, you have the right to request credentials before the individual begins to work with your child. You especially want to know whether he or she has experience with autism. If you are displeased for any reason, report your concerns to the school district before completion of the assessment.

When setting appointments, consider your child's stamina for one-on-one situations. If your child attends to tasks in 10 minute snatches, schedule several shorter appointments rather than a single day-long session. You know her tolerance for frustration best.

You may need a large dose of patience yourself. The testing, report writing, and information collection involved in a school evaluation process can take several weeks, or longer. The case manager then coordinates an acceptable time for a multidisciplinary team meeting. The wait, you hope, will be worthwhile. With reliable, objective evaluation results, your child is one step closer to receiving the appropriate educational assistance mandated by law.

27

INDIVIDUALIZED PLANS

The evaluation team agrees that your child has autism and would profit from special education. The next step is for an education team to plan a special education program tailored to your child's needs.

Special education includes instruction provided by local school districts for children with disabilities. Professionals trained in such areas as hearing impairment or developmental delays deliver these services directly to children and consult with their parents and regular education teachers.

Before your child receives assistance, however, you and the team prepare either an individual family service plan (IFSP) or an individual education program (IEP). Updated versions of these plans guide your child through the education system, so you must understand what the terms involve.

Individual Family Service Plan

Babies found eligible for early intervention services require an individualized family service plan before securing assistance from a publicly funded program. Although the law requires an IFSP for three to five year olds, most early intervention programs prepare an IFSP for children who are newborn to three years old as well.

The IFSP is a written statement of all services indicated for your child's treatment. Areas studied for an IFSP are emotional, social, speech and language, cognitive, sensorimotor, and self-help abilities.

A basic assumption behind the IFSP is the belief that your baby is best served if family needs are met. Accordingly, you may be asked whether you need support with family adjustment, respite care, locating information about autism, or financial planning. From this inquiry, you and the professional team determine a plan that emphasizes methods to support and enhance individual family strengths while giving your child suitable assistance.

The law requires an IFSP review at least every six months. Your participation in the plan ensures ongoing communication. If you want more frequent formal evaluation of your baby's progress, request additional reviews.

Individualized Education Program

An individualized education program (IEP) replaces the IFSP for your school-age child with disabilities. Like the IFSP, the written IEP satisfies several important purposes:

1. An IEP commits the school district to specific resources tailored to your child's learning.
2. The IEP serves as a reference guide for services your child receives that pertain to special learning needs.
3. The recorded IEP functions as an instrument to monitor whether your child actually receives the prescribed services.
4. An IEP is a documented tool to evaluate progress.

Similar to the IFSP process, the school calls an IEP meeting to prepare an educational plan for your child. Your participation is expected for IEP review sessions at least once a year throughout your child's education. Therefore, your recognition of and comfort with the process are vital.

Federal law details who attends an IEP meeting with you. Your child's teacher, or future teacher, a public school representative who has authority for your child's special education program other than the teacher, your child, when appropriate, and any staff member involved in your child's evaluation or education program all contribute to the program plan. In addition, you can bring an advocate, outside evaluator, or interested friend as support or to help you evaluate the program proposed by the school.

The IEP meeting affords an excellent opportunity to meet the people who influence your child's educational future. Each person at the meeting contributes information about current performance. Teachers or therapists relate how they regard your child's behavior. Specialists who assess your child explain their tests and results. Information you contribute about how your child behaves outside school enhances the total picture of your child's progress.

Do your homework before the meeting. Gather copies of past reports, IEPs, and evaluation results, and review them. Target realistic goals. Investigate available programs that benefit children with autism. Ask other parents, or contact your local autism society for recommendations. Observe classes in action to see for yourself whether your child belongs in the program.

Before the IEP meeting, think about what you want to happen, and envision your child over the next few months and coming year. Does your child need speech therapy more frequently to increase communication skills? Would sensory stimulation by an occupational therapist alleviate certain behaviors? Are reinforcers for the behavior management program working? If this is a placement meeting, which classroom best fits your child's needs? Remember to request that a 12-month program be written into the IEP so your child maintains skills learned during the school year.

Go into an IEP meeting prepared and ready to take notes. Bring a tape recorder if you can't record the volume of information that will be shared. Ask questions. Disagree if you understand the facts differently. Share your interpretations. Help the IEP team identify your child's strengths and weakness, and match these qualities with existing district resources or outside services.

This information strengthens the content of your child's individualized education program. The resulting document must include the following:

A statement of your child's present education performance level.

Annual educational goals, or performance one year after the program goes into effect.

Short-term instructional objectives, or gradual steps, to reach long-range goals.

Related support services, such as speech or occupational therapy, to guarantee that your child progresses toward stated goals.

Placement alternatives appropriate for your child. The IEP details such elements as instructional setting, unusual equipment, and group size. It determines the extent to which your child will participate in regular education with nondisabled children.

Projected initiation date and anticipated duration of services.

Assistive devices or support services for your child's learning.

Sign the IEP only after you understand its contents and agree with the recommended services, goals, and placement. If you disagree, you have the option of requesting another review to reassess your child's progress or proceeding with the appeals process. Share your feelings about your child's education, but try to maintain open communication with school personnel—your child's education depends on it.

28

EARLY INTERVENTION AND PRESCHOOL

Almost every source you consult emphasizes the importance of early intervention for children with autism, and for good reason. The first three years of a child's life are critical to later development. Studies consistently demonstrate that early learning benefits all children. For your baby with autism, regular doses of intervention produce significant and long-lasting gains that translate into a brighter future.

What Is Early Intervention?

Early intervention involves special education services for children from newborn to five who have handicaps or who are at risk of developing them. Specific early programs target infants and toddlers and feed older children into school district-sponsored preschool settings. Services range from individual speech therapy to small-group socialization and stimulation.

When early intervention first originated, services concentrated on verifying strengths and weaknesses and planning activities to remedy the gaps. The idea was to minimize losses rather than push beyond preconceived limitations. Following this plan, the child was the main client. Parents received activities to practice at home but were often ignored as part of their child's planning team.

Now professionals understand that babies thrive when family needs are met. Programs view parents as partners in a child's program and progress. A goal of early intervention is to strengthen the parent-child relationship by teaching parents the following skills:

How to feel comfortable with their youngsters
How to structure the home to reduce challenging behaviors
How to practice exercises at home
How to enjoy their child as part of the family

Early intervention programs are conducted at home or in a classroom. Whichever the format, you want someone from the early intervention team to observe your child at home. Home visits are the only way they can see what you deal with and help you structure a setting the family can live with and where your child with autism can thrive.

During the visit discuss whether your child has sleep, toileting, or other problems that cause unusual stress. These challenging behaviors, along with such factors as family lifestyle, other siblings, and daily routine, are all considered in your child's total plan.

Once a plan is finalized with you, a designated team member helps you integrate your child's behavior management and stimulation activities into the family routine. The staff may make additional home visits to ensure reasonable follow-up. Team members may include an *early childhood specialist*, who understands the development of young children, a case manager, speech pathologist, physical therapist, psychologist, or social worker.

Your child's program may center on play therapy to intrude upon her aloofness and to reinforce social skills, speech therapy to work on communication skills, occupational therapy to regulate sensory information, and parent support. Some programs lend toys, books, and amplification and audiovisual equipment.

Along with individual and home-based treatments, your child needs small-group activities to practice social skills. These settings can be with nondisabled children. Recent studies confirm that children with autism make considerable cognitive and language gains in preschool settings that include children with and without disabilities. (See Key 30.)

How Do I Evaluate an Early Intervention Program?

States vary in the types of early learning programs they offer. Inconsistent quality and availability of programs and uneven staff training mean you may need to be persistent to locate the best choice for your child, that is, if you are fortunate enough to have a choice.

Once again, ask other parents for referrals or contact your local Autistic Society of America. Visit different programs to compare how staff interact with children and their parents. Ask as many questions as you need to determine whether a program is appropriate for your child with autism.

- What is the program's philosophy? Is there a balance between structured learning, skill development, and social learning activities to tap an autistic child's ability to relate, interact, and realize feelings? How does staff plan to deal with challenging behavior? Is parent involvement integral to the operation?
- How will the program be tailored to my child's specific needs? Does it have staff trained to recommend early diagnosis and intervention strategies, plus speech and sensorimotor techniques?
- How often will my child receive teaching? Is the program year around?
- What are your recommendations for behavior management? Are educators willing to coordinate activities with my child's private therapist?
- What will my child be taught? Does the program have flexibility enough to make my child's curriculum functional, realizing there is no one program for every child with autism?
- Does the program offer family support with finances, insurance, respite care, and parent and sibling discussion groups?
- How do you help parents work with their child? Do you come to the home? Is there parent training? How are parents kept informed of progress?
- Is there a cost for services? Is my family eligible for financial relief?
- Are opportunities available for both individual and small-group activities? Are children taught skills in multiple settings to increase the chance of carryover? How will my child interact with nondisabled children?

115

- What is your group adult-to-child ratio? If the ratio is more than 3 to 1, do all the children have autism? Are there more than six children total in one classroom?
- Are there other children like mine, or will my child be the only one unable to attend and left wandering for much of the session? Is integrated placement consistent with my child's chronological rather than developmental age to aid socialization?
- How are sessions structured? Do activities work to identify skills and build on them? Is time spent waiting between activities kept to a minimum so my child has little opportunity to revert to isolated or self-stimulating behaviors?
- How is progress measured? Are behaviors and procedures identified and objectively evaluated at frequent time intervals?
- Do classrooms seem safe? Are there areas free of distraction for times when my child has difficulty paying attention, as well as areas that stimulate interest and play?
- How does the teacher interact with the children?
- Does this program seem to value my child as a unique human being?

What Value Is Early Intervention?

Enrolling your youngster in an early intervention program benefits you and your family. Your child receives intensive therapy that taps into her interests and teaches that paying attention to people is worthwhile.

At the same time, you find support to strengthen your possibly shaky confidence as a parent of a child with special needs. Program staff can help you acquire the close, satisfying relationships experienced by any parent and child. Together you plan realistic goals based on your and your child's successes.

29

MOTIVATE YOUR CHILD TO LEARN

"If parents could just spend time it would work out," recommends one adult who overcame many extreme symptoms of autism. "My parents had faith in me, and I wanted to prove I could do better."

Your child wants to prove he can improve, also, but he needs your continued support. Some parents mistakenly believe that once school begins they can rest from coordinating their child's treatment. Indeed, the shuttling from preschool to therapists may end now if your child's program is under one roof. You still need to monitor progress, however, and continue formal and informal home sessions started during early intervention. Through your motivation, your child will gain the confidence to become as self-motivating as the young man who was interviewed.

Several recommendations from Key 21 pertain to encouraging your school-age child as well. These additional suggestions may generate constructive sessions with your older child.

Organize Learning One Step at a Time

One way to motivate your child is to make learning understandable. Establish what is useful for your child to learn, such as putting on pants independently. Then, divide this job into simple steps, such as laying the pants flat, holding the waistline with both hands, sticking in the left foot, and so on.

Present the first step with clear and easy instructions. Show and tell what you want done. Then, instruct your child to comply. To reduce confusion, use the same familiar phrase each time you give the request.

Allow enough time for your child to respond. If a response never comes, provide a *prompt*, or guidance to help your child begin. Your initial request is actually a verbal prompt. Now your child needs you to move him physically through the activity.

Offer a prompt after one verbal command. If you say the same instructions repeatedly without a response, your child learns to ignore your initial requests. Repeat the instruction as you move your child through the activity so he learns the language of what you expect. Praise, or reward, him for following your direction even if you physically prompted the response. Gradually, offer less physical assistance until your child completes the task upon verbal request.

Once your child performs the first step, go on to the next. Confirm that your child understands and performs each step before moving to the next. Test learning by instructing your child to repeat all the known steps from the beginning. Very soon your child will master the entire task independently.

Professionals call this breakdown of learning *task analysis*, and it forms the basis for programs you may encounter called *systematic* or *data-based instruction*. The method applies to most situations, from dressing skills to job training. You probably use task analysis unconsciously every day, such as when you prepare a meal or clean the car. Your child with autism, however, requires this type of organization to understand and complete those steps of a project you perform naturally.

Another way to teach the sequential steps of a task is backward. For example, place your child's pants almost in place, and instruct him to pull the pants completely into place. You might say, "Put on your pants."

Praise your child for following directions. Then pull the pants slightly lower on his leg and repeat the same command. Continue the process with pants dropped lower on your child's legs each time. When they are completely off and your child puts them on with a simple verbal command, he knows the skills independently.

By learning steps backward, your child practices the movements of pulling on his pants and knowing the correct final position.

Apply Principles of Learning

Motivating a child is easier if you understand the underlying premises that influence every learning situation, whether formal or informal. Consider these principles as you structure opportunities to enhance your child's learning.

> Children associate events that are presented at the same time and in the same place. For example, a child understands the concept of putting on pants better if he hears and repeats the direction *and* performs the activity.
>
> Children find it easier to learn information that fits together. For example, letters from a word are usually easier to remember than scrambled letters.
>
> Children tend to learn what they practice. For example, your child may need to role-play a job interview many times before feeling comfortable with the social skills expected in that situation.
>
> Children repeat what they find satisfying and lose interest in what they find unpleasant. Your child will want to duplicate actions that are fun or result in praise, hugs, toys, or other rewards.

Nurture Your Child's Self-Esteem

Children with autism who became independent adults credit supportive people for giving them the confidence to persevere. Whatever your child's functional level, the most important gift you can give is the ability to believe in himself. You already furnish a secure home and diverse experiences. You allow him choices and responsibility. Show your child you respect and appreciate him as a person:

- Remember to offer "please" and "thank you" as you encourage him to speak.
- Discuss misbehaviors in private, if possible, rather than in front of others.

- Knock before entering his bedroom or other private place.
- Involve him in conversations.
- Permit him the opportunity to respond without your prompting or answering for him.
- Introduce him to people you meet.
- Look at him when he speaks to show your attention.
- Recognize his efforts, no matter how small.
- Tell him something positive each day.

Your faith and persistence enable your child to form a better sense of who he is. With this confidence, he develops the motivation to learn and mature.

30

~~~~~~

WHAT ABOUT INCLUSION?

Our culture assumes youngsters will grow into solid citizens who contribute to society, yet the very people who hold these expectations set up a society in which some children are kept separate, particularly those with disabilities. How can these children accommodate to their environment as adults when they receive limited exposure to people and situations through their education? Even the most loving and supportive home cannot afford all the experiences required to live independently outside the home. Children with autism need training in the real world.

What Is Inclusion?

After decades of debate, lawmakers called for the education of children with disabilities in the least restrictive environment. Educators were forced to agree that the best training for life comes from education in classrooms with nondisabled peers.

Over the years, the concept earned a variety of names: *inclusion, regular education initiative, inclusive schooling, mainstreaming,* or *integrated classrooms.* Whichever term your district uses, the basic principles are the same:

1. Teach a child in the neighborhood school along with brothers and sisters, friends, and neighbors.
2. Provide education in a setting with the same access to resources and events as peers without identified disabilities.
3. Receive an education in regular education settings whenever appropriate. This does not guarantee full-time integrated placement or imply that every child belongs fully integrated from the start. However, it is a goal to work toward.

School districts offer different models of inclusion. Your child may learn all or part of a school day in a regular preschool or public school classroom. Her regular education teacher may receive assistance from an aide or therapist. This person works with your child in the classroom or in another room.

Some districts organize *resource rooms*, separate classrooms with a special education teacher who provides a homeroom for children who have one or more particular disabilities. Resource teachers either teach one group all day or spend part of the day with their students in the regular education setting. They help children adapt while offering suggestions to the regular education teacher.

Special education teachers are similar to other teachers, but they plan for a child's total development. Your child's special education teacher incorporates social, communication, and self-help skills into the regular academic program.

Arguments For and Against

School districts vary in their determination to integrate children with disabilities, even though this is the law. Some attempt inclusion only if behavior problems are minimal. Others resist mainstreaming for a variety of reasons you should be prepared to counter.

> *Parents of children with disabilities fear a loss of special services and teachers and worry how children in the mainstream will treat their child.*
> Studies show that children with autism generally make considerable communication and social gains as result of integrated placement. Classmates model language and entice these children into stimulating activities that replace repetitive and antisocial behavior. Regular IEP meetings ensure that valuable services continue when needed. Children and parents also develop relationships that connect them with the local school and community where they belong.
>
> *Administrators from cooperative special education districts worry about their jobs if too many children transfer into local programs.*

Sound inclusion programs need trained special education staff to support mainstream initiatives, wherever they are administered. Inclusion makes sense financially because it eliminates the cost of duplicate services. It allows a single education system that values all students.

Teachers of integrated classes are anxious they will be unable to cope with unfamiliar disabilities.
Urge the school district to provide ongoing special education support for your child's teachers. Once teachers develop new skills, they gain the confidence to realize that inclusion reduces fears and biases. Teachers learn to look past labels and promote respect for the individuality of every child. Everyone becomes more tolerant when teachers treat all students like they belong.

Parents of nondisabled children are concerned that mainstreamed children will consume a disproportionate share of the teacher's time and attention.
Schools employ a variety of innovative strategies for balancing needs in an integrated class. Teachers have aides, appoint peer tutors and buddies within the class, and have support from principals for extraordinary behaviors. Some parents accompany their child to class to ease the transition. Volunteer these alternatives.

Studies indicate that nondisabled children become more accepting and responsible when sharing a class with children who have disabilities. They learn that special needs children are people with feelings who are smarter than they thought previously. Everyone in the school learns that all students, including those with disabilities, are people first.

Pros and Cons for Your Child

Whichever attitudes the local district upholds, your first priority is your child. She may thrive in an integrated setting, benefit from waiting a few months or years for inclusion, or always profit from special education on a full- or part-time basis. Ideally, your local district is flexible enough to tailor a program that meets her needs.

Such groups as The Association for Persons with Severe Handicaps push for total inclusion of every child, but you may not agree that large classes or overstimulating environments would benefit your child now. Evaluate the pros and cons of inclusion for your child by finding answers to the following questions:

- What benefits will my child receive from an integrated setting?
- Does the proposed setting have a diverse curriculum that matches my child's level of development and accounts for the emerging level of maturation?
- Will my child receive the continued behavior management program she needs to control explosive and self-destructive behavior?
- Can my child receive special services? How will these services be coordinated with the integrated program?
- How can I remain involved with my child's program?
- Is my child's program considered individually or part of a set policy, such as integration for gym and art only?
- Does the integrated setting offer opportunities to interact socially with nonhandicapped peers?
- Does the integrated setting provide the skills necessary for postschool adjustment into a community program?
- How will my child be kept productively busy in the integrated setting to reduce wandering and repetitive behaviors?
- Does my child's program consider inclusion in typical activities that let her know she is truly part of the mainstream, such as class pictures, field trips, and a locker near the integrated classroom?
- Has my child continued in the current setting long enough to adjust and for the team to suggest change realistically?
- Has the integration plan been carefully planned and orchestrated? How will students in the mainstreamed class be prepared for my child? How will she be prepared for inclusion, if this involves another school or classroom?
- Is integration frequent enough to be meaningful?
- Will the teacher and support staff have preparation for a child with autism? What ongoing special education supports will the teacher receive once my child is in the class?

- Does the mainstream teacher have preconceived notions about what my child can achieve?
- Is the teacher sincerely interested and willing to work with my child and special services staff?
- Does the mainstream teacher emphasize the individual differences of each student?

Selecting a program that suits your child can be difficult. Inclusion has many faults, but the benefits outweigh segregated alternatives. Decide what your child needs now, but be open to changes in the future.

If you hear your child is the best in the class, you know it's time to switch classes. Stay actively involved in your child's education, and keep pushing for more integrated real-world settings. As one parent emphasizes, "You're dead with complacency!"

31

▲▲▲

ASSISTED COMMUNICATION

Throughout time, people have adapted various devices to enhance and enrich their lives. Today, technological advances provide many creative choices for people with autism. The most exciting application of assistive technology to autism, however, involves communication.

What Is Assistive Technology?

To guarantee equal access to technology, lawmakers passed the Technology-Related Assistance for Individuals with Disabilities Act of 1988 (Public Law 100-407). The law defines *assistive technology* as any specially designed, modified, or commercially available item, equipment, or product system that aids or improves functioning for individuals with disabilities. A broad range of technology falls under these guidelines, from eyeglasses to sophisticated computers.

Because scientists constantly devise new technology, the legislation also funds state centers to monitor and disseminate information concerning technology and disabilities. Centers with government-sponsored assistive technology projects exist in almost every state, usually through state vocational, rehabilitation, or education departments.

Centers act as clearinghouses for data regarding types of equipment, manufacturers and vendors, financial assistance, and programs offering technical guidance. Additionally, Innotek, the technology division of National Lekotek, offers parents and children computer classes, activities, and software lending. (See "Resources.")

Assistive Technology and Communication

For children unable to speak or benefit from sign language, technology offers an array of communication alternatives. The type of device to investigate depends upon your child's level of functioning and how this technology fits his current communication and education program.

A common aid for nontalkers is a communication board. Electronic message boards can be as simple as pressing color-coded yes and no buttons or as complicated as educational software programs involving higher level concepts.

Certain children with autism naturally take to computers as a means of communication. They can spell words on a letter keyboard beyond their apparent capabilities. These mysterious talents form the premise behind facilitated communication, the process whereby a facilitator physically assists someone with a disability to communicate by communication board with words or pictures on a standard or modified typewriter.

Voice synthesizers enable computers to say what the child types, and adapted screens attached to a computer monitor allow easier viewing of messages. The combination of hearing and seeing sounds, words, sentences, and concepts helps many young children learn to talk and read. Adaptive keyboards of all sizes, touch-sensitive screens, and power pads connected to keyboards allow young children with multiple disabilities easier access to conventional keyboards.

Other Benefits of Technology

Some educators dismiss computer-assisted learning for children with disabilities as a fad. Your child with autism, however, may be someone who blossoms with these motivating tools. Computers afford a whole new world of recreation and learning opportunities. These devices are unemotional and nonjudgmental. Operators are in total control because they work independently and at their own rate. If you find your child enthralled with computers, playing time can be adopted as a reward in a behavior modification program.

An unexpected benefit results when children with autism play computer games with children who are nondisabled. The computer becomes an equalizer, or bridge, for social learning, particularly in mainstreamed classes. Advanced skills can translate into adult vocational training. Computer and keyboarding skills are excellent for the adult with autism who never gained social competence for jobs requiring more interpersonal skills.

What You Can Do to Assist Communication

Besides computers, you can engage in other activities with your nonspeaking child to stimulate communication.

- Create your own communication board. Initially, use pictures of familiar people, toys, foods, or objects your child recognizes. Categorize the pictures in rows as you add more. Label each picture so your child connects pictures with words. One parent suggests placing pictures on the surface of a lunch box.
- Speak in short, direct sentences. Your child understands in a very concrete way, so you need to make directions clear.
- Work on developing one-word responses to label objects first, and slowly build from there. If your child is unable to say words, offer something desirable as reinforcement and reward any approximation of eye contact or sounds. Combine manual gestures, prompts, and touching with words that stand for objects to increase understanding.
- Show a picture and ask what it is, once your child knows words for objects. You can also show a picture or object and have your child find another in the room. This activity develops the ability to generalize concepts, which is difficult for most children with autism.
- Talk about everything your child does, will do, and just did.
- Expand what your child indicates or says. For example, your child says "Mumu," and you interpret, "Yes, you want milk."
- Perform an action with a favorite toy in front of your child and hand the toy to your child, or sit facing him and give directions to perform an activity. For example, "Clap your hands." Physically prompt the action if your child needs assistance.

- Repeat what you just asked your echolalic child, adding a quick yes or no at the end, and see if you get a response for or against what you proposed.
- Eat a desired food in front of your child but don't offer any until your child gives you eye contact or utters the sound or word you request.
- Prepare a chart of your child's activities for each day, and discuss them throughout the day.
- Play talk shows on the radio as your child rests so he hears language.
- Send notes to school that repeat what your child did on the weekend or at night, and ask the teacher to talk with him about these activities. Ask for news from school, too. Most people normally discuss their day: it's important to talk about your child's life, too.
- Tell stories that prepare your child for social situations. Some children with autism handle more abstract information when it is written. Create stories with your child that tell about his life.
- Read to your child every day. Ask which book he prefers. If your child seems uninterested, keep reading. Eventually, he will snuggle beside you to read together. Ask him questions about the story once you have his attention.
- Play audiotapes and sing together.
- Take your child everywhere. Allow him to choose foods he names at the grocery and to select a book or treat afterward.

Be persistent even without obvious results. Your child needs time to practice and process the communication messages you offer. Many parents report that once communication is established their child becomes easier to handle. As one parent says, "Change won't happen overnight, but it can happen with time and love."

32

DEVELOPING
ACCEPTABLE
INTERESTS

C hildren with autism are often very good at keeping busy. The problem is the stereotyped or isolating activities they choose to fill their unprogrammed time. They rarely explore the range of leisure and recreational activities open to most youngsters and adolescents. Consequently, they may miss opportunities to discover interests that contribute to a balanced lifestyle.

When you consider that children average between 55 and 75 hours of free time each week and adults have 35 unplanned hours, you understand the importance leisure plays in a person's life. To function independently as adults, individuals with autism must learn to use free time wisely. Start now to help your child develop satisfying pastimes.

Where to Begin
Your child will enjoy the same range of activities as other children. The difference is that she may need more direction to find something interesting enough to hold her attention in a meaningful way.

One place to start is with any fixation, or extreme interest, your child already has, such as cars, maps, or radios. Temple Grandin's autobiography credits much of the recovery for high-functioning individuals with autism, like herself, to committed companions who helped them redirect fixations into constructive activities. Your child could start a collection, read or write about the topic of interest, listen to music, build models, or draw. Finding purposeful outlets could take some creativity on your part, depending upon the fixation.

If your child seems generally indifferent, provide a variety of experiences on varying occasions to see what triggers her curiosity. Remember to try what other children like, such as sports, books, crafts, dress up, music, and baking. Talk with your child's teachers for ideas. The law intends that the individualized education program address unique leisure needs as well as academic goals.

Identifying Options

A good place to experiment with various toys and activities is the National Lekotek Center. Lekotek means "play library," and the organization has play libraries with trained staff around the world to support your child's play explorations.

She can play with conventional and unusual toys at the center or borrow materials to take home. Many Lekotek centers include Compuplay, a technical division. Compuplay sponsors drop-in sessions, classes, and summer camp for children with disabilities who are interested in computers.

Inclusion opens many doors to local leisure and recreation programs that were once closed to individuals with disabilities. These classes and other organized activities often generate lasting interests. As with other outings, you have nothing to lose and your child has another experience to gain.

- Special education cooperatives frequently administer after-school, weekend, and summer recreation programs. Should your child enroll, observe whether someone tries to involve her. For example, if your child refuses to run relays at camp, she can keep score or hold flags at the finish line.
- Park districts run a wide range of classes, lessons, and team sports. Some programs are cooperative efforts with the school special education district, which means the district may be able to provide a companion for your child's participation without disrupting the program. You may want to find someone on your own to accompany your child.

- Libraries arrange story hours and reading-for-fun programs for every age group.
- Zoos and museums offer tours, classes, touching times, and special activities.
- Girl Scouts and Boy Scouts now have groups with disabled and nondisabled members. Because these groups are usually small, activities can be adapted to individual capabilities. You can be part of the mainstream, too, by being a scout leader.
- Very Special Arts conducts programs and training sessions in drama, dance, music, literature, and visual arts for individuals with disabilities throughout the United States and worldwide. Youths share accomplishments in the arts through exhibitions and workshops.
- Special Olympics sponsors individual and team sports education and competition for children and adults with disabilities. The program began with Eunice Kennedy Shriver in 1968. Shriver noticed that her campers with mental disabilities had the physical capability to perform greater feats than acknowledged previously. The original Chicago Olympics went so well the idea spread to 50 states and more than 100 countries worldwide.
- Unified Sports evolved from Special Olympics and the trend toward integrated activities for youth with disabilities. This program pairs athletes with and without mental retardation for training and competition on the same sports team. Find out about local Special Olympics and Unified Sports activities by contacting the national headquarters in Washington, D.C. listed in Resources.

Remember to keep asking your child what she enjoys. Build on these interests. If possible, promote a balance between solitary activities and those that are fun with playmates. Satisfying pastimes are more than luxuries for children with disabilities. They are part of the prescription for a healthy, independent life.

33

FRIENDSHIPS

R esearch indicates that the greatest concerns among people with disabilities involve loneliness and lack of friends. Indeed, many parents report they are extremely saddened by their child's inability to make friends. Even when a child with autism wants to approach people, inappropriate social behavior and communication difficulties may interfere with forming meaningful relationships. This isolation intensifies with age, greater awareness of others, and movement from school to community programs. Everyone needs a friend to share the ups and downs of aging, and so does your child with autism.

Building Bridges

Mainstreamed education is a start to helping your child develop friendships. Yet, integrated classes often afford little opportunity for direct contact between disabled and nondisabled children. Without successful interactions, nondisabled peers remain uncomfortable with someone who talks and acts differently. Similarly, the child with autism has few opportunities to practice the skills necessary to mature socially and emotionally. Only through successful shared experiences can children with and without disabilities learn that two people can be different and still have something in common.

Begin to help your child make friends now. He may misunderstand the subtleties of social relationships or picking up other people's feelings, so you must guide him through the most obvious steps. Initiate a climate that helps your child and others feel more comfortable together.

Practice Acceptable Ways to Greet Friends and Strangers

Differentiate levels of friendship, such as family, professionals who work with him, peers, or possibly later a love interest.

Discuss the responsibilities and expectations of friendships, such as playing at your home, sharing, taking turns, and going places together.

Role-play what to say with a friend versus what to say with a stranger. Act out several situations, such as meeting a stranger, date, or salesperson or sustaining a telephone conversation. Offer words to say in each situation, depending upon your child's age. Record the interactions on audiotape or videotape. Review interactions that require good manners, including when to express please, thank you, and excuse me until they become routine.

Reward Appropriate Social Behaviors

Every child changes with age, and so will your child. Mostly, the changes bring better behavior. Some lower functioning children with autism may remain disruptive and relatively nonverbal, but more often adolescents become less destructive and more verbal and affectionate.

Just like nonautistic adolescents, however, your child may go through sensitive stages. A look or comment or a comparison with someone perceived more competent may trigger anxiety, depression, or regression to tantrums. Deal with each issue as it develops to improve your child's chances for socialization.

Suggest alternatives to distracting behaviors, such as hand flapping or pacing. Create acceptable outlets for anxiety before it builds into tantrums. (Refer to Key 22.) Discuss your child's concerns about autism openly, and help him focus on what he can do well rather than weaknesses. Seek counseling for depression that lasts more than a few weeks. If weight or skin eruptions are a problem, consult a physician for a healthy diet or acne medication.

Talk about ways to cope with teasing and name-calling. Let your child know that all children suffer their share of teasing, and it's painful. Help your child understand that children tease because they feel uncomfortable or bad about themselves. This information may be comforting. If not, discuss alternatives, such as ignoring them or finding an activity to keep busy when others make hurtful comments.

Reward appropriate social behaviors, such as when your child shares, wins and loses graciously, or approaches another child to play. Teach which actions are private, such as nose picking or scratching various body parts. Go on regular outings together to practice public behavior.

Provide Opportunities for Developing the Social Confidence to Make Friends

Introduce neighbors to your child, and let them know you are a proud parent. Your honest enthusiasm will reassure others that your child is someone to know. Invite neighborhood children into your home, to the playground, or for a planned outing. As neighbors learn more about your child, they may visit on their own.

Participate in organized community activities for children, if you have time and energy. The YMCA, YWCA, religious organizations, local park district, government social service agencies, or community colleges often arrange group parent-child play programs for young children.

If your community lacks ongoing programs, organize your own play group. Some larger cities have parent networks that share the names of families to contact, or you can call your local Autism Society of America for members near you who may be interested in forming a play group. Try to meet regularly so the children become familiar with one another.

Expand School and Community Relationships Through a Buddy System

Work with your child's teacher to create a pupil-assisted learning program whereby your child participates in planned group activities under the guidance of a buddy, or classmate. Some districts adopt the *circle of friends* concept begun in Canada. With this plan, the teacher and class discuss the mainstreamed child's strengths and decide how they can encourage these abilities. Classmates share responsibility for the child throughout the day. With time, accepting relationships evolve into true friendships.

Another option for older children is a *Best Buddies* or similar program. Best Buddies is a national network of local organizations that match college students with teenagers and young adults who have mild or moderate disabilities. The pair meets at least twice a month. They can talk, listen to music, or watch movies, whatever activities the buddies decide together. The main objective is friendship. To locate your local Best Buddies program, call the national office in Washington, D.C. or contact your local college or university.

An offshoot of this idea for adults with disabilities is *Citizen Advocacy*, a project currently operated by the Rural Institute on Disabilities in Montana. With citizen advocacy, a volunteer agrees to advance the interests and rights of an adult with disabilities. Contact the institute to start a buddy program for your adult child. Finding and implementing these programs may take time and energy on your part, but the social experience is worth the effort to help your child find a friend.

34

ADOLESCENCE AND
SEXUALITY

A disturbing aspect of adolescence for any parent is their child's emerging sexuality. When your child has autism, you worry how someone so socially immature and naive will handle the many physical, mental, and emotional changes accompanying adolescence. With your patience and guidance, however, your teenager will learn to feel more comfortable with this sexual awakening and the responsibilities it carries.

You can prepare your adolescent for change by offering accurate information at a level that is understandable. Explain facts in a simple, concrete, and matter-of-fact way. Be prepared to answer questions as they arise, and review your responses occasionally. Your child may take longer to understand and sort out body changes and their significance.

If you feel uncomfortable discussing private topics, consult the resources in "Suggested Reading" for assistance. Another option is to ask your child's teacher or counselor for materials created specifically for adolescents who understand differently. You can also talk with your support group or call Planned Parenthood, but prepare your child for this special time of life.

Adolescent Changes

Adolescence is often an exciting yet confusing time for young people. Suddenly, a child is thrust into a natural transition that eventually results in adulthood. Through the teen years physical characteristics and sexual feelings develop. Your child will experience these changes, too.

Expect to see the initial signs of physical adjustment during the preteen years, because children with autism develop within the same time frame as other children. The difference is that their social and emotional development may remain immature. Therefore, these young adults require clear discussions of the health and psychological concerns that adolescence may trigger.

Maturing boys need to understand that wet dreams are normal for males. Warn your son about a cracking voice and facial, armpit, and chest hairs. Talk about body odors, and guide him through a structured routine for body care. When the time comes, teach your son to shave. Role-play dealing with these changes and any teasing he might encounter as a result.

Prepare your adolescent daughter for menstruation *before* it arrives. Explain that monthly cycles, breast development, and pubic hairs are natural in becoming a woman. Plan step-by-step procedures for self-care during periods, and help your daughter practice until the process becomes routine. Teach your older daughter breast self-examination. By age 20, take her to a gynecologist to begin regular pelvic examinations. Find a physician who is willing to work with her a few sessions until she feels comfortable enough for examination.

Sex Education

Not long ago, society assumed autism prevented the social closeness that leads to sexual intimacy. As more children overcome symptoms of autism, however, parents realize the importance of equipping them for positive mutual relationships. When you foster this area of development, you prepare your adolescent for full emotional inclusion within the community.

Sometimes, autism causes teens confusion about how to relate, so they miss the nuances of social situations. Their innocent but inappropriate curiosity about their bodies and those of others offend the very people they want to please. Help your teenager learn acceptable social behaviors.

- Urge your youth to participate in mixed male-female social gatherings. Some parents restrict socializing in the mistaken belief that isolation diminishes sexual desires. Consequently, the child misses opportunities for appropriate physical and emotional stimulation because parents deny a key element of the child's overall health.

- Teach what is public and private behavior. Inform your child that clothes stay on, zippers stay zipped, and buttons stay buttoned. Similarly, masturbation is a private action that is unacceptable in public, as is touching their other private body parts or those of others.

- Review acceptable ways to greet people of different ages and familiarity. (See Key 33.) Discuss who can touch, when, and where. Practice ways to say *no*, so someone doesn't take advantage of your child's social weaknesses.

- Consider what you and your teenager think about dating. If dating is in your child's future, talk about expectations from a relationship, what couples do on dates, who provides transportation, and whether the couple requires adult supervision.

Birth Control

Your child with autism may eventually enter into a long-term relationship that leads to sexual relations, or you may want to take some preventive measures before your adult moves into a community residence. In either case, a young adult with autism who is able to live independently or semiindependently within the community requires specific instruction about birth control, AIDS (acquired immunodeficiency syndrome) virus testing, parenting, and accountability.

Because people with autism seem to have normal ovulation and sperm counts, some parents investigate sterilization for their severely involved young adult. Earlier, a common practice in institutions was to perform sterilizing operations on females with disabilities. Today, most states outlaw involuntary sterilization unless a court declares the individual totally incompetent.

Weigh the trauma of misunderstood surgery and resulting hormone level changes against the benefit of conclusive birth control. Contact the local state attorney's office for guidelines in your state, and consult a physician. Consider the risks and benefits, and choose the least intrusive alternative.

Remember to respect your child's rights to a complete relationship. Even though your child may have difficulty expressing feelings, she has the same needs as you to love and be loved and to share the world with someone who cares.

35

~~~~~~

THINKING AHEAD

With autism, every new event can be a major transition, sometimes to the point of crisis. One of the most drastic upheavals for any student, however, is the passage from secondary school to advanced education or employment. When autism is involved, the transition between school and community working and living seems even more extreme. It helps to plan ahead.

Transition Planning

The Individuals with Disabilities Education Act (Public Law 101-476) addresses the difficulties that families face when they try to plan for their older child's future. The law derived from the reality that many special education students and their families are left floundering once high school ends. Even when enough support services exist, many agencies disagree about who assumes responsibility. Now local agencies must program for even the most handicapped student's future *before* they leave secondary school. Lawmakers call this *transition planning*.

Transition planning acknowledges the importance of identifying postsecondary options and services for students with disabilities. It recognizes that preparation for participation in these programs cannot happen overnight. Skills must be built into educational plans while the student is still in school.

Transition planning follows a format similar to that observed for your child's education program. The law determines that each transition plan result in an individualized written rehabilitation program comparable to the individualized education program.

Each high school student's transition plan specifies activities and services. The overall plan stresses that schooling be preparation for a productive and independent future. The additional components of an individualized written rehabilitation program recognize the following areas:

1. **Family involvement.** Transition plans arise from your teenager's interests and capabilities. You and your teenager take an active part in the decision-making process. Your continued support ensures that school and community service representatives follow through on what makes sense for your child. If your district resists transition planning or you want support throughout the process, contact the Family Resource Center on Disabilities. They offer individual family assessment and training for enhancing the transition process to improve your child's quality of life.

2. **Long-term community involvement goals after secondary school.** Some teenagers with autism benefit from an advanced education curriculum; others may participate in postsecondary education in a special setting. Besides education and training, realistic assessment of employment options becomes part of the plan. Community involvement also includes the intent to pursue living arrangements outside the home. This area explores the range of residential options and opportunities for recreation and leisure activities.

3. **Meaningful short-term activities that help your child achieve practical community goals.** This area specifies which daily living or vocational skills your child needs for the desired school or employment. For many students with autism, routine lessons still focus on behavior and social skills. Teens with autism particularly need job skills that concentrate on getting along with coworkers, communicating, behaving appropriately, and handling interruptions and changes. Review whether these additional areas should be part of your child's transition plan:

   - Ability to take directions from boss and coworkers
   - Attention span for work
   - Safety awareness

- Good hygiene habits
- Transportation skills
- Time and money concepts
- Dressing skills
- Job interview skills
- On-the-job social skills

4. Agencies responsible for school-community linkages. Your student's future plan may rely on several resources. Therefore, the planning team may include representatives from your family, including your child, school, college services, employment after school, high school work-study programs, and recreational, housing, and rehabilitation services.

Resources differ from state to state, so resolve to be determined. The law specifies that transition planning starts by age 16, although some states begin at age 14. Plans must be reviewed yearly and modified as necessary. Urge the team to locate the right services for your child and to follow up regularly.

Your Role in Transition Planning

Autism assumes a variety of characteristics, many of which progress with age. Therefore, reevaluate continuously which options will help your child achieve the fullest potential. Even if your school district waits until age 16, you can initiate transition planning earlier.

Ask your preteen about natural interests and capabilities. Assess together what jobs are reasonable choices given these skills. Review vocational guides at the library, attend career fairs, and interview community employers to analyze career options. Request vocational assessment from a school counselor or occupational therapist.

Translate findings about your child into practical career alternatives. Determine whether the choices require academic, vocational, or a combination of routes. By high school, you and your teenager will be prepared to participate in a formal transition process that evaluates and reevaluates realistic work options in the least restrictive environment.

To assist with future choices, ask the transition team about government programs that train high school students for work after graduation. Suggest internships, time-share jobs, or part-time employment to experience work in a specific industry.

Expose your child early to the interpersonal and job-related activities that must eventually be mastered. Work toward filling in gaps between current skills and possible future goals. These are the *prevocational skills* required for community living and employment.

Give your child public speaking training to help with conversation skills. Provide early work experiences by assigning your child more tasks at home. Supervise your child in shopping, planning and preparing meals, cleaning house, and washing laundry. Observe how your child uses public transportation, makes change, requests directions, answers the telephone, or understands what to do in emergency situations.

Gradually, increase the responsibility for these assignments. If necessary, divide the tasks into simple components for your child to learn and practice step by step.

Help your child choose courses necessary for entry into jobs, college, or trade schools, depending upon interests and abilities. If college is a reasonable choice, begin making plans by the second high school year. Consult the Resource Guide from the American Association of University Affiliated Programs for colleges and trade schools that offer special academic and living programs to individuals with disabilities. Write for catalogues, applications, and financial aid information. Ask whether special entrance examinations are required, and arrange for your teen to take them.

Early transition planning helps families access what they need from the mix of available community resources. The process of transition planning supports your child's goal for maximum vocational and living independence by building future goals into today's educational program.

36

WWWWWWWWWWWWWWWWWWWWWWWWWWWWWWWWWWWWW

WORKING ADULTS
WITH AUTISM

A t one time, many adults with autism languished in state mental institutions. With little to keep them busy, they regressed to self-destructive and repetitive behaviors. Now professionals recognize that everyone, no matter how severely disabled, has the right to contribute to the community in a meaningful way. A gratifying job enhances any adult's self-perception, and work will improve the quality of life for your young adult as well.

Transition planning may ease the path to employment, but your child may still require vocational guidance after high school graduation. The challenge is to locate employment relevant to your child's individual needs rather than expect him to fit into an inflexible work mold. Chances are that your young adult will require employment in a supported environment. Still, you want a program that commits to training workers for satisfying jobs with nondisabled employees.

When seeking employment options, guard against anyone's preconceived notions about autism limiting your child's opportunities. Individuals with autism demonstrate a range of interests, aptitudes, and capabilities comparable to that of other working adults. Many have unique goals for themselves, even though they have difficulty expressing them. Youth with autism deserve consideration for a variety of jobs.

Vocational Assistance

The main agency for vocational assistance to individuals with disabilities is Vocational Rehabilitation (or Rehabilitation), a nationwide federal-state network that assists eligible adults in defining suitable employment goals and finding jobs.

To determine eligibility, your child requires a medical examination to verify mental or physical disability. The disability must be extensive enough to obstruct employment but open to remediation from existing vocational services. Qualifying examinations are free through Vocational Rehabilitation, although certain services thereafter may have a fee.

Once eligibility is established, a vocational counselor matches training and support services with your child's employment goals. Together you consider workplace accommodations that may make employment accessible, such as a talking computer or varied work hours to match your child's stamina. If appropriate, the counselor recommends federally funded on-the-job training or work-study programs. Counselors in many states conduct job training, placement, and follow-up as needed.

States vary in the amount and type of services they offer. Your community telephone directory lists the rehabilitation or vocational office under local state agencies. There is at least one Vocational Rehabilitation office in each state, usually in the state capital.

Additional vocational assessment and training are available through the Association for Retarded Citizens, state employment offices, and federally funded Job Training Partnership Act and Comprehensive Employment and Training Act programs. Other resources are local colleges, universities, and trade and technical schools that sometimes offer adapted programs for individuals with disabilities.

Employment Alternatives

States offer a wide variety of public and private work settings. The type that is best suited to your child depends upon the extent of disability and the amount of support needed to maintain employment. Generally, the federal government differentiates three employment settings: sheltered, supported, and competitive.

In *sheltered employment*, individuals with disabilities receive services in settings separate from nondisabled employees. These services offer a continuum of options that match a participant's performance.

Work activity centers and *adult day care programs* provide vocational and prevocational training continued from high school. Although there may be some job tasks, participants work without pay. Program emphasis is on reducing inappropriate behaviors and increasing social, communication, and daily living skills.

In *sheltered workshops*, individuals complete simple piecework tasks, such as assembling, packaging, sewing, and collating, that are subcontracted from community businesses. Employees receive a minimum wage on a piecework rate basis. The job is guaranteed, but workers cannot choose what they do. Employees rarely receive preparation for integrated or independent employment, and they have little opportunity for advancement.

Supported Employment

An important feature of supported employment is the ongoing training and supervision for community jobs available to individuals with disabilities. This assistance enables individuals with severe disabilities to adapt to competitive settings with nondisabled peers. Support continues through learning, securing, and maintaining the job or until the individual shows independent job proficiency.

Job coaches often come from state employment agencies and are funded through amendments to the Rehabilitation Act and the Americans with Disabilities Act. Businesses that hire their own trainers or sponsor trainees with disabilities receive significant tax breaks.

Public and private agencies adapt supported employment to their settings through a variety of models. Each offers different levels of training from outside coaches or in-house trainers. With *individual placement,* a job coach supervises one on one until the worker learns the task. The coach gradually withdraws training and supervision, and the employer assumes the standard monitoring role.

In the *enclave model,* an on-site or outside job coach provides training and continued supervision to a small group of workers

147

with disabilities. Workers with more extreme disabilities profit from continuous supervision at a job site shared with nondisabled employees.

Another option for more disabled workers to remain in mainstream settings involves *mobile crews*. Vocational agencies supply a job coach for four to six workers. The coach trains and oversees the quality of a specific service the group provides, such as groundskeeping or office cleaning, as they travel to different job sites.

The benefits of supported employment outweigh those of sheltered situations. Workers receive opportunities to improve behavior and job-related skills beyond work tasks while working in a mainstream setting. Improvement usually ensures the flexibility to move into more integrated and independent situations.

Competitive Employment

A small percentage of youths with autism attain competitive employment. They may receive limited prevocational training and assistance with job placement by a rehabilitation agency. Thereafter, they participate independently in full-time or part-time jobs within integrated employment settings. Their wages and performance should compare to similar performance of nondisabled coworkers.

Nowadays, adolescents with autism enter the world of work with more normalized life experiences than ever before. Youths exposed to a host of behavioral, technical, and programmed job-related skills outshine students of years ago, who were sheltered at home or in institutions. More opportunities and openness for individuals with autism translate into fulfilling jobs, higher wages, and employment beside nondisabled peers.

37

▼▼▼▲▲

HOUSING

A normal part of growing up for any child usually involves leaving home. Your child with autism will expect to live elsewhere, too, if the family works toward this goal together. Promote decision making and risk taking. Encourage independence. Most important, begin to prepare early for this natural consequence of becoming an adult.

Background

Housing options for adults with various developmental disabilities have always been limited. Until recently, families were encouraged to commit their children who were different to institutions. Government transported and housed residents in the few available state-run or private facilities. Most often, individuals with autism left their homes and communities, rarely to return or interact with people outside their protected environment.

During the 1970s, expectations changed, and professionals decided residents would lead better lives in the community near their families. Government agencies released scores of inmates, usually without proper training, community programs, or family assistance. Without appropriate supports, a larger percentage of people with autism than other disabilities either returned to institutions, placed enormous strains on their families, or were sent to unsuitable residences.

Current integration trends support mainstream living arrangements for people with disabilities. Local districts are initiating a range of community-based housing alternatives. These initiatives plus equal access legislation recognize that adults with autism have the right to live as independently as possible near their families.

Even with legislative backing and funding, program options remain at a premium in most communities. Residences specifically for autism are even more scarce and have long waiting lists. Once again, you need your advocacy skills, this time to locate the best housing match for an adult with autism. Since finding the best residence and submitting an application take time, start the search before an emergency robs you of your ability to choose.

Living Arrangements

The interest in community-based housing has generated many creative options for individuals with disabilities. Communities vary in what they offer, however, and how they refer to their programs. Generally, residences differ in the amount of independence and structure they provide.

Intensive care facilities are still an option for severely disabled adults who demand 24-hour supervision. These programs emphasize supervised toileting, dressing, eating, and other daily living tasks in addition to structured classes outside the home or on-site. Smaller residences tend to offer individuals with autism more structure for nonprogram hours than larger institutions. Try to avoid any program that lacks structure to keep your child productively occupied or does not challenge your adult to improve.

Group homes accommodate two to eight adults with disabilities in existing community housing. The number of residents and staff to resident ratios change with state and local government codes. Live-in professional staff supervise individual daily schedules that include outside employment and coordinate shared housekeeping activities. Group homes vary in the amount of independence, direction, and privacy they permit residents. Local government agencies and disability organizations, such as the Association for Retarded Citizens or the Autistic Society of America, sometimes sponsor group homes. The benefits of this type of housing include supervised living in a more homelike setting.

Adult foster care, also called family care or skill development homes, is an alternative to group homes. In this situation, one to five adults with disabilities live with a family trained by the placement

150

agency. The resident becomes part of the family while developing skills for independent self-care, employment, and recreation. Parents often reject foster care because they mistakenly believe it reflects on their parenting failures. When foster care providers understand autism, however, this situation provides the critical training and emotional distance that prepare the adult for independent living.

Supervised apartments provide semi-independent living. A staff person lives with a small group of roommates either in an apartment or in a separate but nearby residence. Residents follow their own schedules independently and work outside the home. The staff person merely inspects the apartment and guides residents through procedures to care for themselves and their home as needed.

Independent living recognizes that some working adults with autism can care for their daily needs, calculate home finances, travel to and from employment, and handle free time independently. A few adults prefer to live with a roommate. Roommates share chores and support each other's triumphs and challenges. Your adult with autism may choose to live alone to lessen the demands for social interaction that is sometimes so painful. Find out if your child qualifies for subsidized or partially subsidized independent housing through the U.S. Department of Housing and Urban Development.

Evaluating Residential Programs

Before you contact any program, consider the type and size of program that seems appropriate for your child. Think about your child's supervision requirements and whether housing should be linked to employment programs or prevocational skill training. Decide whether your adult still requires a strict behavior management program or can schedule her day with minimal guidance. Discuss with your child whether she wants or needs a roommate and whether she feels comfortable cooking, cleaning, shopping, paying bills, and attending community recreation activities independently.

After you devise a list of choices that seem reasonable, take the future resident with you to observe different programs. Ask to visit during active times of the day. Stay for a meal to judge for yourselves what living there would be like. Talk with staff, residents, and neighbors. Once you visit, answer the following questions:

- Is the program focus community based? Do staff encourage residents to lead more ordinary lives within the nonhandicapped community? Are program goals consistent with goals for my child?
- Are the amount and type of supervision suitable for my child? Does the environment foster appropriate behavior?
- What is the residence like? How is the physical setting, including the apartment, building, and furniture, cared for?
- Does the program meet basic physical needs for food, shelter, and privacy?
- Is housing located in a safe neighborhood? Can friends and family visit? Is it near transportation, public recreation, and shopping?
- How do residents and staff interact? Is the atmosphere friendly and homey? Are residents kept productively busy and interacting, or are they allowed to vegetate in front of a television?
- Are house rules fair and flexible? Can my child follow them?
- Does the residence offer professional guidance and employment, social, and decision-making opportunities?
- What are the benefits and drawbacks of this arrangement?

Many of these issues can be addressed with your child's transition team. It is hoped that they can suggest residential alternatives before housing becomes essential for your adult. For additional assistance, contact the state disabilities, rehabilitation, or human services department, or you can contact the disability organizations listed in Resources.

Parents unable to locate acceptable housing or who face long waiting lists may want to organize other parents to open a residence. This type of project takes huge amounts of time and energy to raise funds, buy or rent a home, investigate village building codes, and garner local support. Whether you start your own home or seek placement in existing residences, the secret of success is to start planning early.

38

▲▲▲

GOVERNMENT FINANCIAL AID

I ndividuals with autism may be eligible for financial assistance through government-sponsored programs. Various funding specifically applies to living expenses, health care and treatment, respite care, and any devices necessary for more independent functioning. The problem is in locating the plan that pertains to your child and wading through the bureaucratic maze to receive its protection.

Your child may qualify for one of four major federally funded projects: Supplemental Security Income (SSI), Social Security Disability Insurance (SSDI), Medicaid, and Medicare. Each program is administered through the state Social Security Administration and subject to local guidelines that change frequently. States often vary in the amounts they pay and eligibility requirements, so contact your local Social Security office for the most current facts. Some states conduct eligibility for government-assisted programs through a special developmental disabilities division of their department of rehabilitation.

Supplemental Security Income (SSI) and Medicaid

Supplementary Security Income is a public assistance program that allocates monthly cash payments for food, shelter, and clothing to qualified applicants. The program covers anyone 65 or older, blind, or disabled. According to recent rulings, more children with disabilities under age 18 qualify for benefits.

Medicaid pays for doctor, dental, and hospital bills. Someone is eligible for Medicaid if they receive SSI and are over 65, under 21, or between 21 and 65 but disabled. One disadvantage is that

Medicaid frequently limits costs and requires approval before services can be performed or equipment purchased. Without prior approval the agency sometimes refuses to pay.

Many parents find they are flatly denied communication devices, which should be covered as their child's primary means of communicating. Once they appeal with a prescription from a physician or therapist, however, the claim is accepted. The moral of stories with government agencies is *be persistent* with legitimate claims.

Both SSI and Medicaid programs consider financial need. Therefore, part of eligibility depends upon whether your child is 18 years or older and has access to another income. For someone under age 18, Social Security looks at the family income statement along with the diagnosis that the applicant is medically or physically disabled.

Adults with autism must have little or no income and must also be unable to work or earn adequate salary to live, which the law calls *substantial gainful activity*. The amount of earnings the government allows through substantial gainful activity and still pays as SSI benefits varies with state and agency revisions.

Any assets can jeopardize SSI and Medicaid eligibility, so take care that your child's name is omitted from any direct trusts and inheritances. (See Key 39.) Eligibility for these two programs is important because their benefits fund group homes and other housing options for the disabled.

To apply for either program, bring a family income statement or your adult child's personal income statement in addition to the names and telephone numbers of people who can verify your child's disability, such as psychologist, physician, or vocational rehabilitation counselor. Even with proof of disability, the Social Security Administration may send your child to one of their physicians for confirmation. Any visits at their request may be a nuisance but free to you.

Your child also needs to bring a birth certificate and social security card. You can apply for a card from the local Social Security office any time after birth.

154

Social Security Disability Insurance and Medicare

Social Security Disability Insurance offers monthly benefits similar to Social Security Income. The difference is the requirement for eligibility. SSDI pays benefits to anyone disabled before age 22 who has at least one parent whose employment wages contributed to Social Security. That parent must currently be disabled, retired, or deceased.

Your child's payments under SSDI should continue past age 18 and the death of the qualifying parent. You need proof, however, that your child's medical and income situations are unlikely to change and your child cannot perform substantial gainful activity. When applying for SSDI, bring family employment records and other records that identify your child's disability.

People who qualify for SSDI are also entitled to Medicare. *Medicare* is federal health insurance coverage that is independent of income. Someone is eligible for Medicare safeguards if they are age 65 or older or have certain disabilities, including autism. Medicare pays a percentage of hospital and medical costs that results from inpatient or home care services, including respite.

Another government program, *Qualified Medicare Beneficiary (QMB)*, covers out-of-pocket medical expenses for people who may or may not have Medicare and who are ineligible for Medicaid. With QMB, the state reimburses Medicare premiums, deductibles, and other insurance costs.

When seeking information about these programs, prepare for repeated telephone calls, long waits, and delays in processing applications. With Medicaid alone, government agents handle about 80,000 claims a day that they must follow through a nine-step process. Handwritten or incomplete applications only make the process longer. This doesn't mean you should give up. Instead, keep better records of whom you talked with, when, and what they told you. Follow up regularly until your child receives the benefits permitted under law. Government offices and the confusing programs they administer can be frustrating but not impossible to master.

155

39

▲▲

FINANCIAL AND ESTATE PLANNING

F amilies frequently find planning ahead upsetting. Arranging for the future forces some parents to face the disturbing realization that their child with autism may always be dependent. For others, the problem lies in the prospect of dealing with their own inevitable mortality. These issues are scary for parents and children alike.

Yet, when you prepare for contingencies as a natural element of overall family planning, the process becomes much easier for everyone. Important ingredients of this approach involve investigating cash reserves for today, tax breaks, protection of government assistance, and estate planning.

Relieve Immediate Financial Concerns

Permanent disability can burden the most secure family budget, especially when autism is involved. Your child may need long-term therapy outside the school system or be so destructive that you never go anywhere without a checkbook in hand. Therefore, plan now for your child's unexpected expenses.

Financial analysts usually recommend that families supporting someone with a disability set aside six months of cash for easy access, compared with three months for other families. Place the money in a bank, money market fund, or other investments, if you can. Make sure the program allows retrieval of funds if you need them for treatment, therapy, or an emergency.

Other important considerations involve adequate life, disability, and health insurance. For life and disability insurance, first evaluate the family's financial situation should the primary bread-winner die or become unable to work. Consider who brings in the bulk of earnings and the financial risk without this person. Choose life insurance that covers breadwinners rather than the lives of dependents. Discuss different types of insurance plans that fit your total estate plan with a qualified insurer.

Even the best health insurance has gaps in coverage. Investigate whether your insurance company understands what autism is. Many companies deny or cancel coverage because of outdated definitions that interpret autism as mental illness or a psychiatric problem, which they may refuse to cover. Send biased insurers copies of the latest American Psychiatric Association diagnostic criteria confirming a medical condition, or ask your physician to intervene on your behalf.

Insurance is a reason to be cautious about switching jobs or moving to another state. Some workers experience difficulty converting policies because of clauses that refer to preexisting conditions. Remember to inquire about insurance during the interview process. States deviate in their definitions of disability and the types of assistance they allow, which may affect disability benefits. Before making a move, contact local disability organizations for resources concerning insurance options.

Understand Tax Laws

Recent tax law revisions redefined the range of eligible deductions you can take. Currently, medical expenses must exceed 7.5 percent of your adjusted gross income before you can claim deductions. The good news is you can now take deductions for more expenses related to your child's care, such as dependency care, specialized programs prescribed by your doctor (such as camp or a training workshop for you), communication adaptations, or transportation expenses to accompany your child for care. These expenses must be reasonable and supported by written prescriptions from physicians and therapists.

The U.S. Internal Revenue Service details other tax credits in Publication 503, *Child and Dependent Care Expenses*. Keep detailed records of any expenses throughout the year that you think might be valid, and let an accountant decide.

Plan for the Future Together

Planning ahead is a project for the entire family. Don't assume you know what each person thinks about caring for someone with a disability once you are gone. Your family may need many discussions to sort out answers to delicate questions about dependency care:

- What does the child with autism need now and in the future?
- What support does the community offer?
- How can the family best plan for greater independence?
- Who will be responsible for finances and general supervision of care?
- How does everyone feel about caring for a sibling with a disability? How can the responsibility be shared so that siblings can maintain a normal lifestyle?

These issues involve the fundamental question of *competence*. Evaluate whether your child with autism is capable of making commonplace decisions and those that result in more serious consequences. Then, determine the type of future you want your child to have, considering employment, residence, medical care, and recreation. Your child's competence will determine the strategies you plan for a more independent future.

Write your family's desires for the child with autism into a *letter of intent*. This document serves as guidance for future providers once you are gone. It may include your child's history, including medicine reactions, current status and likes and dislikes, skills, recreation activities, advocate names, treatments that work, and your wishes for future care. Update the letter regularly to keep information current.

Place the letter of intent in an accessible location, such as a safety deposit box, and make sure it is clearly marked. Some parents give copies to other siblings or trusted friends or relatives. Letters of intent are not legally binding, but they help future caregivers better understand and provide for your child with autism.

Another way to assist your semi-independent adult child is to structure a lifestyle that limits the number of decisions to resolve. Arrange for automatic bank deposits of checks from government benefits and wages. Establish procedures for the bank to withdraw payments for rent, electricity, or other regular expenses automatically. Open a joint bank account that requires two signatures— your adult child with autism and a trusted family member or friend—for withdrawal.

For matters of health and safety, designate someone to consult with your adult child and authorize routine or more involved health care. In the event your child is incapable of making everyday welfare decisions, appoint an advocate to oversee financial affairs and monitor living and employment arrangements. All this information can be in your letter of intent.

Prepare an Estate to Protect Benefits

The best way to ensure that your wishes are carried out is to write a will. A *will* is a written legal statement of how you want finances and assets distributed among your children. An important aspect of your will is management of care for your adult child with autism. In this case, the will governs the distribution of your estate in a way that protects your child from losing government benefits. Locate a lawyer who is experienced with disability issues to help prepare your will.

To protect your child with disabilities and be fair to other siblings, you need to understand state laws that govern guardianship and disability benefits. The type of investments and estate you create could threaten your child's eligibility for Supplemental Security Income and medical assistance. Therefore, devise a plan that limits the income and resources awarded in your child's name.

Immediately remove your child's name as beneficiary for insurance policies, pension funds, and retirement programs. Although this may disturb you, keep your child's name out of your will in terms of direct inheritance. Many states seize inheritances left to individuals who receive disability benefits. The money goes into a general fund that has no direct value for your child's care. Advise well-meaning friends and relatives *not* to leave your child direct monetary gifts, either.

Provide for your child with autism by placing money into a trust fund specifically designated for services not covered by government programs. The money may go for recreation, extra education and rehabilitation, dental care, snacks, or an advocate—anything but the food, shelter, and clothing funded by SSI.

If your lawyer recommends that you formally disinherit your child with autism, explain to your children that this is only a formality. Your child will receive an equal portion of the estate through a trust that safeguards other benefits.

Select a guardian or trustee to administer the fund. Appoint two or more guardians to divide responsibilities, if you have several children or other qualified and interested parties. The care of someone with autism is a family affair. By planning together, all family members feel more comfortable with decisions about their future.

40

~~~~~~

MAINTAINING A HEALTHY DISTANCE

At some point, parents must admit their job is done, even for a child with autism. This doesn't mean becoming uninvolved with their adult child; it merely means letting go.

Most parents understand that all of their children will eventually leave home when they are ready. You prepared your child who has autism with all the training, guidance, future planning, and love you could give. Recognize when the time is right to distance yourself from this adult child, too.

View Your Child as a Competent Person

Many parents have difficulty viewing their children as self-reliant adults, no matter how competent they are. With autism, the view becomes more distorted because parents may have assumed their offspring will always be childlike.

Professionals claim that these beliefs stem from the continuous pull and tug associated with raising someone who took so much energy. On one side some parents labor to arrange an easier life for their child, hoping the disability will disappear. On the other side they struggle to accept the person as he is. As feelings somehow balance, however, most parents gain a better perspective of their child as independent of the family.

Respect Self-determination

Your adult may experience life in a different way, but he still wants to feel valued as a human being. Self-confidence is crucial to successful independent functioning. Support your child's self-determination through your actions:

- Include your adult with autism in family decision-making sessions. Ask his views, especially about issues that concern him. Demonstrate that you value his opinions.
- Offer choices rather than bark orders as if your adult were a child. Studies show that requests are granted more often and without incident if choice is part of the bargain. For example, the choices can be between two actions or the time to carry out a request.
- Encourage assertive behavior. Reward social interactions that indicate your child's involvement in the real world.
- Acknowledge efforts toward a goal in addition to final results.
- Applaud your child's attempts at survival skills.
- Allow your child time to adjust away from home without interference.

Remain Active in Your Child's Life

Even after your child moves away from home, someone may still need to oversee that his programs are fulfilling their obligations. Now your job as parent changes from caregiver and chauffeur to manager and supporter. Work with services to help employees understand your child better, and monitor progress regularly but from afar:

- Evaluate whether your child seems happy.
- Ask if he participates in community and household activities.
- Inquire if his work seems satisfying.
- Assess whether the community living arrangement is offering sufficient food, clothing, and shelter.

Discuss any concerns with your child. If a problem exists, contact the staff person at the residence. If you still aren't satisfied, notify the social service agency that sponsors your child's community and employment placements. Your child is entitled to live and work in settings that help him feel content and worthwhile.

Continue to Be a Family

Distancing yourself from your adult children means accepting that family members have different relationships. The physical distance between each other forces you to connect as adults who respect each other's freedom and decisions. Even though you live apart, however, you remain family.

As you adjust to your new lives, you discover that you still enjoy each other's company. Maintain regular contact with all your adult children. Call, write, or visit, but never unannounced unless your children approve. Encourage siblings to socialize without you. Spend holidays and special days together as you would with any family members.

Let the professionals sort out the mysteries of autism. You and your child enjoy the lives you shared together and now share apart.

QUESTIONS AND ANSWERS

What is autism?

Autism is a developmental disorder characterized by a cluster of behaviors. The areas most affected are communication, behavior, and social skills. These, in turn, can influence maturation in other areas of functioning.

Did we cause our child's autism?

The exact cause of autism is still a mystery. During the 1950s and 1960s, theorists blamed parents for what they assumed were psychological problems causing a child's autism. Modern researchers, however, cite several different origins of autism. Studies support that varying forms of autism come from brain damage, nervous system injury, viral infections, genetic conditions, or chemical imbalances. All these options suggest a biological cause for autism. None of these theories suggest bad parenting or that you or your partner did anything to cause your child's symptoms.

Will my child outgrow autism?

Children with autism display a variety of symptoms. More often some form of these symptoms persists throughout life, making this a lifelong condition. Because researchers have yet to find a common cause of autism, they lack the knowledge to discover a cure. The characteristics of autism usually lessen with age and consistent treatment, however. A small percentage of children with autism achieve total independence as adults, with few remaining characteristics.

Will my child have normal intelligence?

To date, research suggests that about 70 percent of children with autism have some form of retardation. This figure is based on an intelligence quotient (IQ), which is calculated from formal achievement test norms. About 10 percent of children with autism excel in isolated skills, such as music, mathematics, or memory. These characteristics are called savant skills, and they may be seen in combination with severe deficits in other areas.

A better predictor of a meaningful life, however, is your child's ability to function independently within the community. Try to keep an open mind about what your child can accomplish. You may be surprised by the changes that result from early treatment and consistent education.

What is the best treatment for autism?

There is no one treatment for all the symptoms of autism. Treatment plans must be individualized to suit your child's unique makeup. The only general treatment to stand the test of time and effectiveness is a *structured* (predictable rather than rigid) educational program that manages behavior with behavior modification and targets goals to individual functional levels.

Should my young child live at home or in an institution?

Because early theorists blamed parents for their child's autism, treatment usually involved removing youngsters from their home and placing them in institutions. Since the trend away from institutions began in the late 1970s and autism became known as a biological condition, researchers discovered that children who lived with their families thrived beyond previous expectations. Adults with autism who were raised at home developed fewer stereotyped behaviors and had greater communication skills than those raised in institutions. They were better prepared to work and live in community residential settings.

With even more opportunities available today, your child with autism can actively participate in your family and community

165

education, recreation, and work programs. Find out what family supports are available in your area by contacting organizations noted in *Resources*.

Can my child learn?

Even if you find poor performance on intelligence tests or you hear a diagnosis of mental retardation, your child can still learn. The difference is that the rate of learning may be slower. Autism may also contribute to inconsistent learning in one or more areas.

Will I have another child with autism?

The incidence of autism ranges from 5 to 15 per 10,000 births. Of these children, between 2 and 3 percent will have siblings who show similar symptoms and another 10 to 15 percent who have significant learning difficulties.

A genetic component of autism is found in fragile X syndrome. Parents with a child who has this genetic abnormality and is autistic have a 50 percent chance of having another child with autism. Only 10 percent of fragile X cases have autism, however. Talk with a geneticist about giving your child with autism a blood test to rule out fragile X syndrome or other hereditary conditions that contribute to autism.

What type of lifestyle can I expect for my child with autism?

Expect that your child will lead an independent life within the community as an adult. Prepare your child to live, work, and fill leisure time productively. The degree to which your adult child will need social supports to carry out these goals is difficult to predict. The best you can do is provide a loving home that fosters positive self-respect. With this motivation, your child will feel content and worthwhile—the hope for any human being.

GLOSSARY

Adult daycare adult programs that provide prevocational training in segregated settings.

Adult foster care community residential placement for one to five adults with a family trained in disabilities.

Americans with Disabilities Act (ADA) of 1990 legislation that prohibits exclusion of anyone on the basis of disability.

Amniocentesis medical procedure to test abnormal chromosomes by withdrawing fluid from the uterus.

Anticonvulsant medication to control epileptic seizures.

Antipsychotics common class of medications that suppress the action of dopamine, a chemical that transmits impulses between nerve cells.

Asperger's syndrome a condition with social abnormalities similar to those in autism but with normal intelligence and language development.

Audiologist trained clinician who tests for hearing loss.

Auditory integration training treatment that retrains the sense of hearing by gradually desensitizing the ear to certain unpleasant sounds.

Auditory memory ability to recall information that is heard.

Autism behavioral syndrome that affects communication, social relationships, and behavior.

Autistic-like characteristics of autism that occur with other disabilities in the same child.

Aversive therapy controversial treatment involving physical punishment to reduce self-abusive or destructive behavior.

Behavior modification strategy that uses rewards to reinforce acceptable behavior and punishment for discouraging behavior.

Best Buddies organization that matches college students with teens and young adults who have mild to moderate retardation for the purpose of friendship.

Case manager coordinator of an interdisciplinary team who manages diagnostic or early intervention services to families.

Cerebellum portion of the brain that controls mental and motor tasks.

Child psychiatrist medical doctor who studies behavior and learning, dispenses medicine, and evaluates reactions to medication.

Children's Justice Act (Public Law 99-401) and **Children with Disabilities Temporary Care Reauthorization Act (Public Law 101-127)** legislation that approved grants for states to develop and implement affordable respite care programs and crisis nurseries.

Chorionic villus sampling (CVS) medical procedure for analyzing chromosomes in a fetus between 8 and 11 weeks by withdrawing cells from the maturing placenta.

Chromosomes particles that make up each gene.

Circle of friends program concept in which mainstream classmates take responsibility for befriending a child with disabilities.

Citizen advocacy project operated by the Rural Institute on Disabilities in which a volunteer agrees to advance the interests and rights of an adult with disabilities.

Cognition ability to store and process information.

Communication skills development of speech, language, or gesturing to transmit messages.

Competence ability of an adult child with disabilities to make commonplace and more serious decisions.

Competitive employment full-time or part-time employment in a mainstream work setting without social service support.

Comprehensive Employment and Training Act (CETA) federally funded employment program.

Developmental disability pervasive influence on development.

Developmental scales checklists that compare a young child's progress with that of other children of the same age.

Diagnostic and Statistical Manual of Mental Disorders (DSM-IV) diagnostic criteria devised by the American Psychiatric Association that differentiates autism as a physical disorder.

Dopamine chemical that transmits impulses between nerve cells.

Early childhood specialist professional trained to understand the development of young children.

Early intervention programs services for children aged newborn to five who have handicaps or are at risk of developing them.

Echolalic language that repeats, or *echoes*, what has been said by someone else.

Education for Handicapped Children Act (Public Law 94-142) legislation that guarantees free public schooling for children with handicaps.

Education of the Handicapped Amendment of 1986 (Public Law 99-457) amendment to Public Law 94-142 that establishes incentives for states to serve all children from ages three to five with disabilities.

Electroencephalogram (EEG) examination that produces a visual record of electrical impulses discharged by brain cells.

Enclave model employment option in which a job coach provides training and continued supervision to a small group of workers with disabilities at a job site with nondisabled workers.

Epilepsy involuntary seizure activity caused by electrical discharges of the brain.

Expressive language ability to use words, symbols, and gestures to communicate with others.

Eye-hand coordination ability to organize eye and hand movements necessary to pick up tiny objects, as in eating, dressing, and writing.

Facilitated communication technique in which a trained professional, or *facilitator*, guides a person's wrist as they type letters into a computer keyboard to communicate.

Fenfluramine medication being studied to reduce levels of serotonin in the blood.

Fine motor skills body movements using small muscles involving the hand and fingers.

Fragile X syndrome newly identified syndrome with weak X chromosome that is the second leading cause of mental retardation and a possible cause of 10 percent of autism cases.

Genes message centers in human body cells that account for growth, development, and physical characteristics.

Genetic disorder error in the message centers of the body's cells.

Geneticist scientist trained in the study of human genetics.

Gross motor development body movements using large muscles.

Group homes residences that accommodate two to eight adults with disabilities in existing community housing.

Inclusion practice of integrating individuals with disabilities in settings with nondisabled peers.

Independent living living arrangement in which an adult with disabilities lives in the community without supervision.

Individual family service plan (IFSP) written statement of services a young child and family will receive from an early intervention program and how these services will be evaluated.

Individualized education program (IEP) written statement of the special education and related services a child requires for learning.

Individualized written rehabilitation program (IWRP) written transition plan that identifies necessary skills and agencies to prepare a student for adjustment into the least restrictive community programs after secondary school.

Individuals with Disabilities Education Act (IDEA) (Public Law 101-476) amendment to the Public Law 99-457 that requires states to establish programs for children aged three to five, to investigate alternatives for children younger than three, to pay for assistive devices, and to plan the transition from school to adult programs for individuals with disabilities.

Infantile autism symptoms of autism that include social, behavior, and communication deficits that occur before age three.

Intelligence quotient (IQ) computation made by comparing standardized test scores with national norms.

Intensive care facility 24-hour supervised residence for severely disabled people.

Interdisciplinary team group of specialists from different disciplines who offer diagnostic and treatment services.

Jargon language specific to a particular group or professional specialty.

Job Training Partnership Act (JTPA) federally funded employment program.

Least restrictive environment term designated by law to indicate the education setting most integrated with nonhandicapped children.

Letter of intent document written by guardians about the child with disabilities that serves as guidance for future providers.

Limbic system structures within the cerebellum portion of the brain that regulate emotion and behavior.

Mainstreaming practice of including individuals with disabilities with nondisabled peers in such settings as school and work.

Medicaid government assistance to qualified people for doctor, dental, and hospital bills.

Medicare federal health insurance coverage independent of income.

Mental retardation slower rate of development.

Minor tranquilizers class of medications prescribed to reduce anxiety that are generally ineffective for symptoms of autism.

Mobile crews four to six individuals with severe disabilities who offer a variety of services to employers as a team and are supervised by human services personnel.

Multidisciplinary team education professionals from different disciplines who evaluate a child's functional level and progress.

Neuroleptics (major tranquilizers and antipsychotics) class of medications that suppress the action of the chemical that transmits impulses between nerve cells.

Opoids brain chemicals that regulate pain perception and motivation.

Options approach treatment based on an intrusive program of unconditional acceptance of a child's behavior.

Oral-motor functions use of the tongue, lips, and jaw.

Pediatrician medical person interested in a child's overall development.

Pediatric neurologist medical specialist who investigates the brain and nervous system in children.

Perseverate repeat the same behavior endlessly.

Pervasive developmental disorder (PDD) general term that emphasizes the range of deficits caused by autism.

Placenta sac protecting the fetus.

Positive reinforcement reward for appropriate behavior that increases the likelihood that behavior will recur.

Prevocational skills instruction in tasks and social skills required for employment.

Prompt help someone to begin an activity or carry it through.

Proprioception input from the brain to muscles and joints.

Psychologist professional who studies human behavior and learning.

Qualified Medicare beneficiary (QMB) federal medical insurance assistance that covers out-of-pocket medical expenses for people who may or may not have Medicare and who are ineligible for Medicaid.

Receptive language facility to understand words, symbols, or gestures.

Rehabilitation Act of 1973 (Public Law 93-112) first legislation to mandate that public programs create opportunities for individuals with disabilities or lose funding.

Resource room separate classes for full-time or part-time instruction with a special educator whose activities support students with special needs and their regular education teachers.

Respite care rest from the responsibility of caring for someone who has a disability offered by an individual familiar with special needs children.

Savant individual with an isolated, outstanding skill.

Self-help skills activities of daily living required for independent care.

Sensorimotor skills large and small muscle movements and visual coordination of these actions.

Sensory integration therapy treatment based on touch and movement activities that help a child organize the senses to react with the outer world in a functional manner.

Serotonin chemical in the blood found in 33 percent of people with autism and thought to affect social skills.

Sheltered employment work setting that isolates individuals with disabilities from nondisabled employees.

Sheltered workshop employment setting in which workers perform industrial subcontracting piecework tasks in a location separate from nondisabled workers.

Social and emotional skills sense of self and ability to interact appropriately with others, leading to total well-being.

Social Security Disability Insurance (SSDI) federal monthly assistance to anyone disabled before age 22 who has at least one parent whose employment wages contributed to Social Security and is currently disabled, retired, or deceased.

Social worker coordinator of social services from an interdisciplinary diagnostic team who works with families.

Special education instruction provided by local school districts for children with disabilities.

Speech and language pathologist professional who assesses hearing and evaluates characteristics of speech and language.

Standardized tests measurement of intelligence based on assessment of thinking skills applied to general knowledge and compared against norms for other people the same age.

Substantial gainful activity legal term for the ability to work or earn adequate salary to live.

Supervised apartment semiindependent living for a small group of roommates with disabilities who are supervised by a staff person who checks on the group regularly.

Supplementary Security Income (SSI) public assistance that allocates monthly cash payments for food, shelter, and clothing to eligible applicants.

Supported employment competitive employment in a mainstreamed setting that offers ongoing support to adults with disabilities.

Syndrome cluster of common behaviors.

Task analysis division of a task into understandable components to teach one step at a time.

Technology-Related Assistance for Individuals with Disabilities Act of 1988 (Public Law 100-407) law guaranteeing access to items, equipment, or systems that can maintain or improve a child's functioning.

Transition planning identification of community involvement goals, services, and activities for a student after secondary school.

Vestibular sense how the body moves through space and changes head position.

Vocational rehabilitation national federal-state network that assists eligible people with disabilities in defining suitable employment goals and finding jobs.

Voice quality resonance, pitch, articulation, and fluency of speech or other verbal communications.

Voice synthesizer assistive technology that enables computers to say what someone types.

Will written legal statement of how finances and assets are to be distributed among children to manage care for a child with disability.

Work activity center prevocational unpaid work setting that concentrates on acquiring social and daily living skills.

DEVELOPMENTAL SYMPTOMS OF AUTISM*

C hildren with autism may show some of these signs. The range of symptoms broadens with age, although certain symptoms ease or disappear with maturity and effective intervention.

Symptom	0–18 Months	1.5–4 Years	4+ Years
Social skills	Avoids eye contact	Avoids eye contact	Lacks imitation skills
	Resists cuddling	Rejects comforting	Treats people like objects
	Remains detached from main caregiver	Prefers to play alone	Shows no awareness of people or their feelings
	Smiles late or not at all	Lacks imitation skills	Chooses to play alone
	Rejects efforts to comfort	Seems unaware of other people	Resists physical affection
	Stiffens body when picked up	Fails to take turns	Lacks appropriate emotional and social responses
	Plays alone		
	Uninterested in baby toys		

---

*Source: Adapted from the Autism Society of America brochure, 1991, and "The Importance of Early Diagnosis in Autism," the Autism Society, Ontario, 1993.

Symptom	0–18 Months	1.5–4 Years	4+ Years
Communication	Lacks nonverbal communication Rejects others' attempts to communicate Imitates no gestures Lacks gurgles, babbles, or first words	Exhibits delayed language Unable to understand language Lacks suitable gestures Says unusual first words Echoes language Talks with unusual speech	Displays delays in language Uses little expressive language Fails to initiate conversation Makes unusual sounds and comments Repeats what others say Uses pronouns improperly Talks in unusual voice quality and pitch
Sensorimotor	Stares for extended periods Repeats body movements, such as hand flapping or rocking Reproduces simple actions with objects Resists changes in routine or surroundings Has delayed motor development Is overactive or extremely passive Responds unusually to sensory stimuli	Manipulates body and objects in unusual manner Attaches inappropriately to objects Shows distress for no discernible reason Resists slightest change in routine	Is preoccupied with narrow interests Has extreme need for sameness Insists on following rigid routines Attaches to unusual objects Is preoccupied with twirling or flapping items

176

Symptom	0–18 Months	1.5–4 Years	4+ Years
Self-help	Displays problems eating and sleeping Is overactive or extremely passive Responds unusually to sensory stimuli Explores little Refuses to chew on solid foods	Shows extreme fear Fights sleep Has difficulty with toilet training Displays no fear of real dangers	Injures self Displays uneven independence in dressing, toothbrushing, and bathing Overeats favored foods Refuses to try new foods
Cognitive			Displays unusual rote memory or savant skills Shows little meaning behind unusual skills Exhibits inability to generalize learning Has difficulty with abstract thinking

WHAT OTHERS WANT TO KNOW ABOUT YOUR CHILD

General Information

Pregnancy and birth history

Family history of delayed language, medical or psychological problems

Medical history, including allergies and inoculation dates

Developmental milestones, such as walking and talking

Diagnostic and assessment test results

Therapy reports

Individualized education plans (IEPs)

Early intervention and school reports

General Observations

Is your child aware of surroundings and people? How do you know?

Does your child follow a routine?

How does your child react to daily activities, such as eating, sleeping, bathing, and dressing?

How does your child react to change and new experiences?

What does your child prefer to do?

What does your child dislike doing?

What motivates your child? What would be a good reward for your child?

Who motivates your child? Does your child have a favorite person or people?

How long can your child attend to an activity?

Does your child's energy level vary during the day?

Does your child tire easily?

Which are peak periods for attending and learning?

Which are the worst times to introduce an activity?

Is your child on any medication? For what reason? How is it working?

Has your child had any health problems? When and what type?

Observing Your Baby (Birth to Age Two Years)

Communication

What types of sounds does your child make? At what age did you first hear them? Are there specific circumstances when you hear these sounds, such as when your child is happy, uncomfortable, or playing independently?

Which activities seem to trigger sounds?

Does your child look at you when you speak or make sounds?

Does your child respond to a name?

Does your child try to imitate speech sounds or words?

Does your child have an unusual ability to count or recite nursery rhymes and television commercials? Do these seem to replace regular communication, or are they repeated at inappropriate times?

Can your child put words together to make simple sentences?

Does your child have an alternative form of communication, such as pointing or pantomime?

Sensorimotor Skills

Does your child seem to hear and see adequately?

Does your child react differently to information presented visually, aurally, tactilely, or by motion, such as swinging or spinning? What is this response?

Does your baby like to be touched and held? How do you know?

Which position does your child prefer for play—lying on back, side, stomach, upright, or sitting? Which position does your child prefer for resting?

Do loud or strange sounds startle your baby? Does your child turn the head toward sounds?

Does your child reach for objects or point to items that may be of interest?

How does your child hold and look at objects?

Does your child prefer one hand over the other?

How does your child position the body for different activities, such as resting, playing, and moving?

When did your child lift the head, roll over, sit, crawl, walk, run, jump, or climb stairs? Is there anything unusual about the way your child accomplishes these tasks?

Does your child imitate movements?

Does your child perform an unusual action, repeated for a period of time, such as hand flapping?

Social and Emotional Skills

Does your child prefer to play alone or with other children or adults?

Does your child reach out to you?

Does your child seem alert?

Is your child generally happy?

Is your child persistent?

Does your child look for objects or people once they are out of view or reach?

How does your child react to frustration, pain, or happiness?

Observing Your Child

Communication

Does your child indicate *yes* and *no*?

How does your child make needs known?

Can your child imitate phrases or simple sentences?

Does your child follow simple commands, such as Give me the ball, or Put the block in the box?

Does your child initiate conversation?

Does your child reverse I and you when responding to a communication?

Does your child say inappropriate things at inappropriate times or repeat the same few comments as conversation?

Sensorimotor Skills

Does your child have any unusual fine or gross motor skills?

Does your child have good balance?

Can your child copy simple shapes?

Can your child build a tower with blocks?

Does your child use scissors, crayon, paintbrush, and pencil? What does your child do with these objects?

Does your child favor one hand for activities?

Does your child seem to learn better when information is presented visually, aurally, or tactilely?

Do your child's vision and hearing seem sharp?

Does your child have any unusual fixations?

Cognitive Learning

Does your child recognize or express basic concepts and qualities, such as hot-cold and same-different?

Can your child name objects from the house and community?

Which activities hold your child's attention? For how long?

What has your child learned recently?

Is your child obsessed with letters or numbers or a particular subject or project?

What is your child interested in learning?

Does your child have an unexplained fund of knowledge in a specific area?

Is rote learning used to replace communication?

Social and Emotional Skills

Does your child follow established rules?

Can your child wait for turns?

How does your child play with other children? Is your child teased frequently?

Does your child pretend or have imaginative play?

Does your child have friends? How do they interact?

How do you reward your child?

How do you deal with inappropriate behavior?

How does your child act away from home?

How does your child take winning and losing?

How does your child handle frustration, and how is it expressed?

Does your child have bizarre mannerisms?

Does your child understand and respect others' privacy and property?

Can your child show and express emotions appropriately?

Self-help

Does your child assume any family responsibilities? What household chores does your child complete?

How does your child handle free time?

How does your child handle toileting at home and in public places?

Does your child eat independently with utensils and acceptable table manners?

Is your child aware of appropriate clothing for the weather and occasion?

Can your child dress independently, fastening zippers, buttons, snaps, laces, and hooks?

Does your child participate in washing, bathing, hair care, and toothbrushing routines?

Can your child stick with a task until completed?

TIPS TO ENCOURAGE SLEEP AND TOILET ROUTINES

Sleeping

Develop a time for bed and a routine, and stick to them.

Organize a pleasant and welcoming room for sleeping.

Allow your child to take a comforting object to bed.

Buy a night-light to lessen fear of the dark, or leave a light on in a nearby room. Your child may enjoy a fish tank. Fish have a hypnotic effect, and tanks have lights.

Play soft music at bedtime to block out ringing in ears.

Provide bed covers that can act as a cocoon. Let your child sleep in layers of clothing, under layers of blankets, or in a sleeping bag to minimize bombardment by tactile stimuli. Earmuffs or headphones may provide a barrier to unpleasant night sounds.

Set toys by the bed to occupy your child should he awaken at night.

Devise a plan for withdrawing from a child who has difficulty separating from you at night. Say goodnight, and tell your child you will return in a predetermined time, such as five minutes. Return at the appointed time for a quick reassurance and leave for another five minutes. Continue the process until your child is asleep. Gradually, extend the time between check-ins. After a week or two one goodnight will be sufficient.

KEYS TO PARENTING THE CHILD WITH AUTISM

Set a timer so your child has the reassurance of sound that you are around and will return in the allotted time.

Lower the crib mattress for young nighttime wanderers.

Awaken a child who is frightened by a nightmare to reassure her that the dream was not real.

Use a heating pad to warm cold linens.

Place your child in a hammock to sleep to provide motion so she doesn't need to bang her head.

Allow your child with autism to share a room with a younger sibling, who can become a role model for bedtime routines and company at night.

Place a buzzer under a rug by your child's bed for when he leaves the bed at night.

Drive your child around in the car until he falls asleep, if all else fails.

Toileting

Develop a behavior plan for training. For a few days, chart when and how often your child eliminates. Once you establish a pattern, devise a toileting schedule surrounding times your child is most likely to need the bathroom. Follow a set routine for toileting procedures that includes dropping pants, wiping with toilet paper, replacing pants, flushing, and washing. Praise your child for any toileting behavior at first, including sitting still. Reward him for every urination or bowel movement in the toilet. Expect him to clean up messes, although you may have to prompt the activity. Otherwise, keep reactions to a minimum.

Have your child record dry nights and/or positive bathroom experiences on a calendar chart. Buy stars or fancy stickers. Ignore accidents, but watch the stars increase.

Desensitize the child who is scared of bowel movements by first rewarding a bowel movement completed in a diaper but in the bathroom. Then reward sitting on the toilet and having a bowel movement. Once your child is comfortable on the toilet and eliminating, cut a hole in the diaper. This way, she can have a bowel movement without toilet water splashing her, which upsets some youngsters.

Buy a child seat that fits inside the adult toilet seat to block water and accustom your child to the toilet. Leave a step stool near the toilet if your child is short or bothered by the height.

Secure a device that causes an alarm to ring if your child passes urine in bed. The alarm awakens your child so she can finish urinating in the toilet or child seat.

SUGGESTED READING

General

Baron-Cohen, Simon, and Patrick Bolton. *Autism: The Facts.* Oxford: Oxford University Press, 1993 (good overview of autism but limited in practical techniques).

Clayman, Charles, and Jeffrey Kunz. *American Medical Association's Children: How to Understand Their Symptoms.* New York: Random House, 1986 (overview of development and health care for all children).

Frith, Uta. Autism: *Explaining the Enigma.* London: Basil Blackwell, 1990 (interesting but technical analysis of autistic characteristics).

Gerdtz, John, and Joel Bregman. *Autism: A Practical Guide for Those Who Help Others.* New York: Continuum Publishing Company, 1990 (insights into family dynamics relating to autism).

Gerlach, Elizabeth. *Autism Treatment Guide.* Eugene, OR: Four Leaf Press, 1993 (overview of approaches to autism).

Kozloff, Martin. *Reaching the Autistic Child*, 2nd Edition. Champaign, IL: Research Press, 1993.

Peschel, Enid, Richard Peschel, Carol Howe, and James Howe. *Neurobiological Disorders in Children and Adolescents.* San Francisco: Jossey-Bass Publishers, Number 54, Summer 1992.

Powers, Michael, ed. *Children with Autism: A Parent's Guide.* Rockville, MD: Woodbine Press, 1989 (practical and comprehensive overview for parents in understandable language).

Wing, Lorna. *Autistic Children: A Guide for Parents and Professionals*, 2nd edition. New York: Brunner/Mazel, 1985. (one of first insightful overviews with practical information about autism for parents: some ideas old-fashioned but still useful).

Medical and Assessment

American Psychiatric Association. *Diagnostic and Statistical Manual of Mental Disorders* (DSM-IV). Washington, DC: American Psychiatric Association, 1994 (diagnostic criteria physicians follow to determine autism).

Bailey, Donald, Jr., and Mark Wolery. *Teaching Infants and Preschoolers with Handicaps.* Columbus, OH: Merrill Publishing Company, now Macmillan (Columbus OH 43216), 1984 (offers guidelines for assessment situations).

Buyse, M. L., ed. *Birth Defect Encyclopedia.* Dover, MA: Center for Birth Defects Information Services, 1990 (genetic information).

Wodrich, David. *Children's Psychological Testing: A Guide for Nonpsychologists.* Baltimore, MD: Paul H. Brookes Publishing Company, 1984 (reviews commonly used developmental scales and screening instruments).

Young Children and Their Challenges

Jones, Sandy. *Crying Baby, Sleepless Nights.* Boston: Harvard Common Press, 1992 (ideas to deal with sleep problems).

Segal, Marilyn. *In Time and with Love.* New York: New Market Press, 1988 (excellent for understanding development and providing activities parents can do with their babies).

Siblings and Friends

Meyer, Donald, Patricia Vadasy, and Rebecca Fewell. *Living with a Brother or Sister with Special Needs.* Seattle, WA: University of Washington Press, 1985 (excellent, easy-to-understand book for siblings and parents).

Perske, Robert. *Circles of Friends.* Nashville: Abingdon Press, 1989 (excellent discussion of how to ensure individuals with disabilities build lasting friendships).

Powell, T., and J. Gallagher. *Brothers and Sisters: A Special Part of Exceptional Families*, 2nd edition. Baltimore, MD: Paul Brookes, 1992.

Personal Accounts

Barron, Judy, and Sean Barron. *There's a Boy in Here.* New York: Simon & Schuster, 1992. (mother and son tell story of son's emergence from autism).

Grandin, Temple, and Margaret Scariano. *Emergence: Labeled Autistic.* Novato, CA: Arena Press, 1986 (amazing personal account of one woman's path to overcome autism).

Hart, Charles. *Without Reason: A Family Copes with Two Generations of Autism.* New York: Harper & Row, 1989 (moving account of brother and son with autism).

Kaufman, Barry. *Son Rise.* New York: Harper & Row, 1981.

Kaufman, Barry. *A Miracle to Believe In.* Garden City, NY: Doubleday & Company, Inc., 1981 (Kaufman's options approach of unconditional love and how it helped his son and others).

Park, Clara Claiborne. *The Seige.* Boston: Little, Brown and Company, 1982.

Williams, Donna. *Nobody Nowhere.* New York: Random House, 1992 (moving account of a woman's development through autism).

Financial Planning

Russell, Mark. *Planning for the Future.* American Publishing Company, P.O. Box 988, Evanston, IL 60204-0988.

Turnbull, H. R. III, A. P. Turnbull, G. B. Bronicki, J. A. Summers, and Gordon Roeder. *Disability and the Family: A Guide to Decisions for Adulthood.* Baltimore: Paul Brookes, 1989.

Adolescent Issues

Dayee, Frances. *Private Zone.* Edmonds, WA: Charles Franklin Press (teaches children skills to prevent sexual assault).

King County Rape Relief. "He Told Me Not to Tell." 305 South 43 St., Renton, WA (parent's guide for talking with children about sexual abuse).

Marks, E., and A. Lewis. *Job Hunting for the Disabled.* Hauppauge, NY: Barron's Educational Series, 1983.

NCCAN Clearinghouse. *Child Sexual Abuse Prevention.* P.O. Box 1182, Washington, DC 20013 (tips for parents about discussing sexual abuse prevention).

Scheiber, B., and J. Talpers. *Unlocking Potential: College and Other Choices for the Learning Disabled.* Bethesda, MD: Adler and Adler, 1987.

Smith, M.D. *Autism and Life in the Community: Successful Interventions for Behavioral Challenges.* Baltimore: Paul Brookes, 1990 (assessments and processes for integration into community living, working, and social programs).

Assistive Technology

Apple Computer Company, Inc., and Trace Research and Development Center, University of Wisconsin in Madison. *Apple Computer Resources in Special Education.* Allen, TX: DLM Teaching Resources, 1989.

Biklen, Douglas. *Communication Unbound: How Facilitated Communication Is Challenging Traditional Views of Autism and Ability/Disability.* New York: Teacher's Press, 1993.

Magazines and Newsletters

The Advocate. Autism Society of America, 8601 Georgia Avenue, Suite 503, Silver Spring, MD 20910.

The ARC. Arlington, TX: Association for Retarded Citizens (association newsletter available to members that discusses issues related to retardation and advocacy).

Autism Research Review International. Autism Research Institute, 4182 Adams Avenue, San Diego, CA 92116.

Dialect. 3031 Louise Street, Saskatoon, Saskatchewan, S7J3L1, Canada (comprehensive bimonthly newsletter dealing with disabilities).

Exceptional Parent. Boston, MA: Psy-Ed Corporation and University of Boston, School of Education (published eight times a year for parents of children with disabilities).

Inclusion News. Centre for Integrated Education & Community, 24 Thome Crescent, Toronto, Ontario M6H2S5, Canada (useful newsletter discussing all aspects of mainstreaming).

Journal of Autism and Developmental Disorders. Plenum Publishing Corporation, 233 Spring Street, New York 10013.

The Map (More Advanced Autistic Person). 3701 West 108th Place, Crown Point, IN 46307, (219) 662-1311 (deals with issues affecting individuals with autism who are high functioning).

For Young Readers

Amenta, Charles A., III. *Russell Is Extra Special: A Book About Autism for Children.* New York: Magination Press, 1992 (good explanation of how one family deals with autism: primary grade picture book).

Dick, Jean. *The Facts About Mental and Emotional Disabilities.* Mankato, MN: Crestwood House, 1988 (explains special needs to children in grades 1 through 5).

Gold, Phyllis. *Please Don't Say Hello.* Human Sciences Press, 1984 (preachy but informative story for 8 to 11 years).

Katz, Illana, and Edward Ritvo. *Joey and Sam.* Northridge, CA: Real-Life Story Books, 1993 (picture book about two brothers, one with autism).

Martin, Ann. *Inside Out.* New York: Holiday House, 1984 (story of a boy with a younger brother who has autism: 8 to 12 years).

Martin, Ann. *Kristy and the Secret of Susan.* New York: Scholastic, Inc., 1990 (Baby-Sitters Club story of a new baby-sitting charge who has autism: 8 to 11 years).

Moss, D. Lee. *Lee, the Rabbit with Epilepsy.* Rockville, MD: Woodbine, 1989 (4 to 8 years).

RESOURCES

C heck directory assistance to request new numbers for government agencies that seem to change with administrations.

[Key: (+) referral/information; (o) local programs; (x) newsletter/publications; (#) funding source.]

Autism and Mental Retardation

Autism Outreach Project
123 Franklin Corner Road
Suite 215
Lawrenceville, NJ 98648
(609 895-0190 + o x

Autism Research Institute
4182 Adams Avenue
San Diego, CA 92116
(619) 281-7165 + x

Autism Society of America
7910 Woodmont Avenue, Suite 650
Bethesda, MD 20814
(800) 3-AUTISM + o x

Autism Support Center
64 Holten Street
Danvers, MA 01923
(508) 777-9135 + x

National Association for
Retarded Citizens (ARC)
Suite 300,
500 East Border Street
Arlington, TX 76010
(800) 433-5255 + o

General Disabilities and Health Care

American Academy of
Pediatrics
141 Northwest Point Road
Elk Grove Village, IL 60009-0927
(800) 433-9016 + x

American Association of
University Affiliated
Programs for Persons with
Developmental Disabilities
8630 Fenton Street, Suite 410
Silver Spring, MD 20910
(301) 588-8252 + o x

American Speech-Language
  Hearing Association
10801 Rockville Pike
Rockville, MD 20852
(800) 638-8255 (voice/TDD) + x

The Association for Persons with
  Severe Handicaps (TASH)
11201 Greenwood Avenue,
  North
Seattle, WA 98133
(206) 361-8870; (206) 361-0113
  (TDD) + o x

Council of Regional Networks
  for Genetic Services
Cornell University Medical
  College
1300 York Avenue
Genetics, Box 53
New York, NY 10021
(212) 746-3475 + x

Easter Seal Society
70 East Lake Street
Chicago, IL 60601
(312) 726-6200 + o x

ERIC Clearinghouse on
  Handicapped & Gifted
  Children
Council for Exceptional
  Children (CEC)
1920 Association Drive
Reston, VA 22091-1589
(703) 620-3660 + x

National Information Center for
  Children and Youth with
  Disabilities (NICHCY)
P.O. Box 1492
Washington, DC 20013
(800) 695-0285 + x

Roeher Institute
Kinsmen Building, York
  University
4700 Keele Street
North York, Ontario
M3J 1P3, Canada + o x

Treatment Programs
Autism Research Institute
4182 Adams Avenue
San Diego, CA 92116
(619) 281-7165 +
(vitamin and diet therapy and
  research information)

Facilitated Communication
  Institute
Syracuse University
364 Huntington Hall
Syracuse, NY 13244-2340
(315) 433-9657 +
(facilitated communication)

Center for the Study of Autism
2207 B Portland Road
Newberg, OR 97132
(503) 538-9045 + o
(auditory training)

Irlen Institute
5380 Village Road
Long Beach, CA 90808
(310) 496-2550 + o
(visual therapy)

Option Institute
2080 South Undermountain Road
Sheffield, MA 01257
(413) 229-2100 + o
(psychologically based accep-
    tance therapy)

Sensory Integration
    International
1402 Cravens Avenue
Torrance, CA 90501-2701
(213) 533-8338 + o x
(sensory integration training)

Treatment and Education of
    Autistic and Related
    Communication Handicapped
    Children (TEACCH)
CB7180, 310 Medical School
    Wing E
University of North Carolina
Chapel Hill, NC 27599-7180
(919) 966-2173 + o
(education-based program
    training)

Advocacy and
Mainstreaming
Family Resource Center on
    Disabilities
Room 900

20 East Jackson Boulevard
Chicago, IL 60604
(800) 952-4199;
    (312) 939-3519 (TDD) + o x

The Mad Hatters
P.O. Box 2
Kalamazoo, MI 49005
(616) 385-5871 o
(theater group)

Planned Lifetime Advocacy
    Network (PLAN)
104-3790 Canada Way
Burnaby, British Columbia
V5G 1G4, Canada + o

Rural and Military
America Council on Rural
    Special Education (ACRES)
University of Utah
221 Milton Bennion Hall
Salt Lake City, UT 84112
(801) 585-5659 + x

Department of Defense
    Dependent School
Special Education Coordinator
Suite 1500
225 Jefferson Davis Hwy.
Crystal Gateway 2
Alexandria, VA 22202
(703) 746-7867 + o

Rural Institute on Disabilities
University of Montana
52 Corbin
Missoula, MT 59812
(800) 732-0323 (Voice/TT) + o x

Specialized Training of Military
    Parents (STOMP)
12208 Pacific Highway, SW
Tacoma, WA 98499
(206) 588-1741 +

Siblings
National Association of Sibling
    Programs
The Sibling Support Project
Children's Hospital and Medical
    Center
4800 Sand Point Way, NE
Seattle, WA 98105
(206) 368-4911 + o x

Assistive Technology
ABLEDATA
Springfield Center for
    Independent Living
426 West Jefferson
Springfield, IL 62702
(217) 523-2587 +

Alliance for Technology Access
1128 Solano Avenue
Albany, CA 94706
(800) 992-8111 + x

Compuplay and Innotek
National Lekotek Centers
2100 Ridge Avenue
Evanston, IL 60201
(800) 366-PLAY + o x

Disability and Business
    Technical Assistance Center
(800) 949-4ADA (Voice/TDD)
Great Lakes Disability and
    Business Technical
    Assistance Center
University Affiliated Program in
    Developmental Disabilities
1640 West Roosevelt Road
Chicago, IL 60608
(312) 413-1326 + x

Legal Issues and Financial Planning
Commission on Mental and
    Physical Disabilities
American Bar Association
1800 M Street NW
Washington, DC 20036
(202) 331-2200 +

Estate Planning for Persons
    with Disabilities
3100 Arapahoe Avenue
Park Place, Suite 112
Boulder, CO 80303
(800) 448-1071 +

Internal Revenue
Consumer Information Center
Department 92
Pueblo, CO 81009
(800) 829-1040 or
(800) TAX-FORM + x

U.S. Department of Health and
    Human Services
Social Security Administration
Baltimore, MD 21235
(800) 772-1213

U.S. Department of Justice
Civil Rights Division
Coordination and Review Section
Box 66118
Washington, DC 20035-6118
(202) 514-0301 (voice), (202)
    514-0381/83 (TDD) +

Employment and Transition Planning

HEATH Resource Center
National Clearinghouse on
    Postsecondary Education for
    Individuals with Disabilities
American Council on Education
Suite 800
One DuPont Circle
Washington, DC 20036
(800) 544-3285

Respite

Texas Respite Resource
    Network (TRRN)
P.O. Box 7330, Station A
San Antonio, TX 78207-3198
(512) 228-2794 + x

Recreation

Best Buddies
1350 New York Avenue, NW
Washington, DC 20005
(202) 347-7265 + o x

National Lekotek Center
2100 Ridge Avenue
Evanston, IL 60201
(800) 366-PLAY
(international network) + o x

Special Olympics International
Suite 500
1350 New York Avenue, NW
Washington, DC 20005
(202) 628-3630 + o

Very Special Arts
Education Office
John F. Kennedy Center for the
    Performing Arts
Washington, D.C. 20566
(202) 628-2800 + o

INDEX